salmonpoetry

Publishing Irish & International
Poetry Since 1981

the **arts council** an chomhairle ealaíon

funding
literature
artscouncil.ie

Rita Ann Higgins
Our Killer City

isms, chisms, chasms and schisms essays and poems

Published in 2018 by
Salmon Poetry
Cliffs of Moher, County Clare, Ireland
Website: www.salmonpoetry.com
Email: info@salmonpoetry.com

ISBN 978-1-912561-09-4

Cover Photography: *'Galway Graffiti' by Jessie Lendennie*
Cover Design & Typesetting: *Siobhán Hutson*
AUTHOR PHOTOGRAPH: *Andrew Downes*

Printed in Ireland by Sprint Print

Salmon Poetry gratefully acknowledges the support of
The Arts Council / An Chomhairle Ealaíon

In memory of my son in-law
Pat Mackey
who died 9th August, 2017

In memory of my friend
Mary Dempsey
who died on 7th November, 2018

Acknowledgements

Some of these pieces or versions of them have previously appeared in Rita Ann Higgins' *Sunday Independent* 'This Woman's Life' column.

The essay "Manifesto" was published in *The Poetry Review* in 2017. It was commissioned by the editor, Emily Berry.

The essay "The Lost Land" was commissioned by Jody Allen Randolph, editor of a special edition of *PN Review* celebrating Eavan Boland's 70th birthday.

The poem "No One Mentioned the Roofer" is from *Ireland is Changing Mother* (Bloodaxe Books, 2011. www.bloodaxebooks.com).

The poems "Work On", "The Power of Prayer", and "The Benevolent Coat Saver" are from *Throw in the Vowels: New & Selected Poems* (Bloodaxe Books, 2005. www.bloodaxebooks.com).

The poem "Our Killer City" was first published Galway's *City Tribune* in 2017.

The poem "Capital of Cock-a-Leekie Inferno (9 Circles of 2020 Hell)" was first published in Galway's *City Tribune* in 2018.

The poem "It Suits A Narrative" was first published in *New Writing from Ireland: Celebrating 250 Years of Hodges Figgis*, edited by Alan Hayes (Arlen House, 2018).

The poem "Looking Out from the Fog" was first published in *Even the Daybreak: 35 Years of Salmon Poetry*, edited by Jessie Lendennie (Salmon, 2016)

RTE Radio 1's *Sunday Miscellany* recorded a version of the essay "Lake Garda."

RTE Radio 1's *Arena* broadcast a version of the essay "The Seamstress with the Syntax" under the title "Memories of a Workshop".

RTE's *Six One News* and *9 O'Clock News* both featured an excerpt of the poem "Capital of Cock-a Leekie Inferno".

Nuacht TG 4 featured an excerpt of the poem "Capital of Cock-a Leekie Inferno".

Special thanks to Jessie Lendennie and Siobhán Hutson of Salmon Poetry, Neil Astley of Bloodaxe Books, Dara Bradley of Galway's *City Tribune* and *Connacht Tribune*, Jenny Farrell, Brendan O'Connor of the *Sunday Independent,* and *Hotpress* magazine.

Preface

I don't know exactly how it happened but I think my poetry book *Tongulish* was sent to *the Sunday Independent* with the hopes of a review in 2016. I had a note from Brendan O'Connor, editor of *Life Magazine* and deputy editor of *The Sunday Independent*. He convinced the big bosses to publish a poem of mine in full from that book. That poem was called "The Mission" about the suicide of my nephew. Shortly after that The Late Late Show rang me and they wanted me to read an excerpt from the poem that they had read in *The Sunday Independent*. A little while after that I had another note from Brendan O'Connor asking me would I think about writing a short column for *The Sunday Independent*. The title of the column was called *This Woman's Life* and it was fortnightly.

It could have a bit of humour, a bit of personal stuff, a few gossipy anecdotes, a bit of deep thinking. I could write about what was going on in the West. I could also occasionally add a poem to the piece if it tied in with it in some way. My first piece appeared in August 2016 and I wrote several pieces up to August 2017. It was never going to be a full-time position because I am a full-time writer and full-time grandmother to my four grandsons. Other pieces in this book come from invitations from editors of literary journals and the like. They don't necessarily go hand in glove with *The Sunday Independent* pieces but they give me the oxygen to proffer different types of writing.

RITA ANN HIGGINS

November 2018

Contents

I

II

I

All About The Base

So we are on the prom in Salthill. The three grandchildren and myself. The nine-month-old twins are in the double buggy babbling and spitting. They are called after two Irish saints, Axel and Cooper. Their cousin, my other grandson Oisín, is seven and like most seven-year-olds he likes to ask a lot of questions. Why do people kick the wall, Mamó? It's an ancient thing, something to do with warts I think. Don't ever let me catch you kicking the wall. OK Mamó. We put on the Pokémon gloves he got on holiday, one each. His one has an annoying noise which can be activated when we snare a Pokémon.

People go all weird when they see twins. Ahh aren't they lovely? Are they twins, I knew they were twins. The questioner wants to know when people know the answer, why do they ask the question? I don't know I think it has something to do with warts and walls. Are they just wasting words? Yes but we have plenty to spare.

I stopped the practice of using the buggy as a weapon (it's called buggy bashing with menaces) when a wheelchair user locked eyes with me at Heuston station and made me feel like Steve Martin in Dirty Rotten Scoundrels. I was bruised and sore for a week, and very resentful. I wouldn't mind but I had lost my favourite coat the same day.

Anyway after our Pokémon hunt we were ravenous. The twins were now chewing the gloves. Nearby hotel, treat, yes please. All settled in and ready for a little banter with the waiter. Is the tap water filtered? 'As in' says he. When anyone says 'as in' it's code for WTF are you on about? I said 'as in' do ye serve it with Cryptosporidium and chips or do ye filter it first and catch all the bad boys? I think they do something with it downstairs, he replied. We gave him our order, a pizza to share and two glasses of tap water. He came back in a few minutes and said the pizza was off. I asked if it was gone off or just off the menu. It's off the menu we were told. We were disappointed, the last time we were here we saw people having pizza and it looked nice. We had talked up a pizza on the prom and we were ready.

Can I see the manager please? I am the manager, he said. This is a four star hotel, I said, keeping my voice low and civil, could the chef not rustle us up a pizza, we just wanted a Margherita (for the love and honour of Christ I nearly said). I'm afraid that is not possible said the proud manager, sticking out his chest toward the Cliffs of Moher. The chef does not make the base here, we buy it in, but today we are all about the base, no trouble and no pizza. So if the base is out it is clear we are not in with a smidgeon of a chance, so we left. The twins were down to three fingers on the gloves. The questioner wondered why they had not put a sticker on the menu to say the pizza was off. I think he has warts or something worse, I said. We ended up going to Lana, the Asian street food place down the road. I sent the questioner in for chicken noodles. We ate them in the car. The twins were spewing carrot-coloured stuff into our hair while we ate. We ignored them completely.

NOTE TO SELF: Send email to City Hall to find out where my fee is for the lovely poem I spent ages writing for them. If they don't hurry up and pay me that's the last time I'll ever do anything for that shower. NOTE TO SELF: Bring back the fountain pen to Powells The Four Corners, it didn't work. Maybe you are supposed to hold it upside down and let the ink drip in like a canula.

* * *

I have a root canal on Wednesday morning. No need for note to self. Oddly it's not something you forget. I'll take two Nurofen Plus before I go in. That's my answer to everything. Before the Angelus, arragh I'll take two Nurofen Plus to take the edge off. Before I watch Vincent Browne, arragh I'll take two Nurofen Plus to steady my nerves when I'm listening to Enda's army.

Galway is full of canals, sadly they are greatly polluted and not helped by all the gunk and worse that is thrown into them every long and short weekend, according to The Galway Waterways Patrol. Most local politicians don't want to hear about the excrement floating in the canals (i.e. shitty city).

Back to my pending root canal. Once you try not to think of something, you are actually telling your subconscious to remember it. You would have a better chance of forgetting it if you said to yourself I'm going to try to remember it, Capisce! I tried not to look it up but I faltered after five minutes and Safari-ed it. It's like liposuction but the hose goes down inside the cavity or canal of your tooth and hoovers the bejasus out of it for about an hour. Then a bit of concrete is put on top of it. You are left weakened and bewildered. As you dander around Galway flaking away, stay away from the canals. Be friendly to your dentist, I say.

I went back to Powells The Four Corners with the fountain pen. The woman behind the counter was warm and energetic. She went in the back and ran it under the tap and she came out shaking it like a wan possessed. A drop of water and a good shake, she said, it works every time, and it did.

What is privacy?

The Minister for Health will come to Galway. Well he might come to Galway. He will possibly come to Galway. There is a good chance that he will come to Galway. There is a fair to middling chance that he will come to Galway. There is a mediocre chance that he will come to Galway. Some say, pigs will fly before he will come to Galway. Others say Donald Trump will perfect and recite a book of Haiku in Irish before the Minister for Health will come to Galway.

To be fair to him or as we say locally, in fairness, The Minister was going to come to Galway. He intended to come to Galway. His visit to University Hospital Galway was imminent. He polished his shoes for Galway. He read all the files about Galway. He knows that patients' lives are in danger in Galway. He knows that the emergency department in Galway is a fireball waiting to happen. He knows about the overcrowding in A&E. He knows that you may trip and break your neck on someone's belongings left beside a trolley; the same patients may now have squatter's rights, they are there so long.

The lack of privacy is embarrassing, to say nothing of humiliating for all involved. You are literally touching off the next trolley. The whole place has a dark ages feel about it. Why should people be dehumanised in this way? Galway is a difficult city to be sick in. We might be the Capital of Culture going forward but going backwards we are the patients on trolleys that the minister forgot. Forget us not minister we implore you. Because we know that when you see the substandard conditions and general state of the place you will close it down.

Dickens himself could not describe the drabness, the dankness, the overall hopelessness that floats in the atmosphere in the emergency department in Galway. Yes, we have a Minister for Heath and he is coming to view the situation in Galway or so we are told. Someone might whisper in his ear (when he does come, if he does come) about the leaked report that states consultants have been accused of failing to take responsibility when things go wrong in the emergency department. The place is being run by overworked nurses. They are not getting paid for all they do. Dignity is not a word that would fit comfortably in any description pertaining to how the patient is being treated in Galway's not fit-for-purpose accident and emergency department. But lack of dignity is a term that will ring out at every turn.

When Pine Martens Do the Siege of Ennis

I used to love to rummage in charity shops. The only thing that changed since I was on The Late Late Show is that I no longer have the same freedom to do that. I'd have no problem holding one sleeve of a jumper and saying to the woman holding the other sleeve, 'back off biatch or you'll get two in the temple' in a *Breaking Bad* voice. I miss that and the way the chutzpah thing works there. Eyes on the prize, you see the jumper, it has your name on it and you go in for the kill. Effrontery is the name of the game.

For this reason I've decided the next time that Tubridy turns up in my garden, shouting up at my window for me to come on The Late Late Show, I'll say clear off outta that and go and get Beyoncé for yourself and leave me to my sleeve tugging war of words with Grindle from Galway. I don't care how much my daughters like him.

A child called to the door asking me would I like to buy a line, I said no thanks and closed the door fairly quickly. I felt a bit rotten about it later on. She couldn't have been more than five if she was that at all. She was probably someone's granddaughter from the street and the real me said, no thanks. Your first response is the true you. Goethe says, we never learn about ourselves by thought but by actions.

This fella I know is a right chameleon, he used to train pine martens to do the Siege of Ennis but he lost interest after one of them attacked him down below. Today in town he intoned that he had a crate of electronic ankle bracelets he bought cheap in Rio and he was selling them on for a song. He was holding them in a bunker near the back of the Piscatorial School in Claddagh, and as they are selling the school he has to move them. Back in the day the Piscatorial School was used for teaching boys how to make nets and girls were taught to sew and spin. I always liked that building; it has character and its own history. It's also a listed building. It stands majestic next to the Dominican Church. My fear is it will end up smothered in flats or be turned into a giant knick-knack shop, or worse. The Dominicans own it and they know the value of C-notes. They are asking €500,000 for it.

A few days later two kids called to the door selling lines. Of course I'll buy a line, I'll buy the whole book and here take this gold watch and here you might as well take the car, I've no need for it. When we have time to think we are all Mother Theresas.

Guilt-free and giddy I headed off to meet the guy about the electronic ankle bracelets. Sure I might as well take a few of them off ya. What harm would it do to have a few, for a rainy day?

Since I had to put the dogs down for throwing the neighbour's python so far in the air he landed on their own electric fence and fried, I've no security at all. At least this way if Marco puts his big hoof over my back wall...

Who's Marco? Marco de Sade, I've hardly a knicker left after him. He's after my shocking pink ones for ages but they are my Cryanair ones and he can't have them. The next time his size thirteen lands in my backyard he'll land in a manacle. How are you so sure? Cos I'll take them all and have them strategically placed that's how. I'm not loving the grey, have ya got the bracelets in any other colour? Did they sort out that ticket touting thing in Rio yet? How long will they get would ya reckon? They'll get nothing but the boxers who put on a couple of bets, they'll be the fall guys. They'll be demonised the length and breadth of the country.

NOTE TO SELF: Never accept an invitation to read at La Salle Secondary School in Ballyfermot, even if they did finally give in and allow Paddy Flynn permission to attend. The fact that he is a traveller has nothing to do with their initial response. My eye. It's who we really are. Back to Goethe, not by thought but by actions do we know ourselves.

A few days later I'm heading out pushing the twins around the estate when I see the little girl and her grandmother. They were waiting for the bus. The grandmother looked at her watch. The little girl looked straight at me.

The Asinine By-laws Department

There is new department in the bowels of City Hall called The Asinine By-laws Department. A banjo of new by-laws is in the making, they have the same appeal as a rusty bucket in a clump of briars. By the time it gets its Capital of Culture crown Galway will have morphed into a police state.

No tree or shrub climbing. How do you climb a shrub? No fence, railing or wall climbing in a park or open space. No cycling, no skateboards, no rollerblades in a park or open space. No citizen shall play football in an open space, better to do it indoors and wreck the capodimonte figurines Granny brought back from the Congo. No flower plucking with or without a pheasant plucker's son, not even one flower or you could face a conviction of up to €1,900.

No pet owner shall be allowed to let their dog have a run without its leash at any time of the day or night. Council staff will be given the power to implement this orthodoxy. These by-laws are against nature, against children and against living. To add to the outrage experienced by the gongoozlers of a sultry evening, there is now a whiff of Gulag in the air.

Next they'll introduce a meter for clocking up flatulence. The more you exude the more you pay. Nearly all of the colourful murals that gave Galway the apocryphal sense that is was a place of welcome for artists have been painted over in a dour distempered cat's melaka grey. One department commissions and pays for a mural, another department (probably just next door) threatens legal action if the mural isn't painted over in jig time. As was the case recently regarding the mural on the former Taaffe's shopfront.

Lacuna (partner of Rio ankle bracelets guy) so called because she fell into the San Andreas Fault during a Pokémon hunt. The dazzle from her lucky bag earrings was seen from space. She was swooned upon and saved by a drone that was arsing around on its half day.

She said they had a consignment of wine tinnies with my name on them. I told her I'd have nothing to do with wine out of a tin. She said out the side of her mouth, 'It wasn't that long ago that you'd drink it out of a slop-out-bucket in Galway's A&E department'. I was tempted to release the Kraken on her but I am saving him for the round-up after Galway's Days of By-law Implementation has kicked in.

There is another nasty coming down the tracks from the Department of the Environment, Community and Local Government. It's called, Open Libraries Pilot Service. It's another name for get rid of library staff and allow people to come in and swipe a bar-coded plastic card and not have any contact with another human. How much is this harebrained scheme saving the Government? Did anyone do research into how it is impacting on people working in Libraries? It has been rolled out in Tullamore, Banagher and Tubbercurry and it's coming to a place near you soon. Sadly Sligo town library is already set to close.

A visit to the library and an interaction with a member of staff can be lifesaving for a person who lives on their own. As well as helping to educate us, libraries are part of the fibre of our society that enhances positive mental health. Some genius wants to change the name from Open Library Service to the Oprah style title, My Open Library. It will be My Open Library with no staff to offer a kind word or make a suggestion about a book or help you log on to the internet or help you by just being there.

Next thing you know you'll only be able to get mass via Skype and you'll only be able to get a mass card signed with a digital certificate borrowed from revenue. Your plenary indulgence will land in your inbox aided by a background chorus of winner winner chicken dinner.

In the report about the pilot projects it states that there were very few antisocial incidents and those were of a very minor nature. What does that even mean? Are we back to flatulence again? The spin is that this harebrained scheme does not affect staffing levels. Balderdash. Surely the whole psychology behind it is to cut costs by getting rid of library staff.

Staffless libraries could prove to be a dangerous place for vulnerable members of society. There will be no toilet access during staffless library hours as this is an area that cannot be monitored by CCTV. Oh but don't worry, you can dial an emergency number if someone sticks a knife in your ear, but not if you live in Offaly; there you ring a security firm. I'm sure there is a duty of care to our citizens that is not being adhered to with this ill-considered scheme.

I might see reading as a gift and a privilege, because it gives me so much pleasure and for me it's the best learning tool. It should be neither, it should be a right. Your right, my right, our children's and grandchildren's right. John McGahern said, 'I see reading and writing as completely related, one almost couldn't exist without the other.' You can almost hear his voice saying that.

A few weeks ago I was asked by Ruth Webster of Books Upstairs in D'Olier Street, if I would sign a copy of *Tongulish* for a customer of theirs who lives in the States. She had forgotten to ask me when I read there earlier in the year. I signed the book and sent it to her and today in the post I received from Ruth a gift of a book of literary essays called, *The Fun Stuff and other essays* by James Wood. The essays range in subject from *Homage to Keith Moon* to Sebald's *Austerlitz* to essays about the brilliant Marilynne Robinson and Lydia

Davis (of Flash Fiction fame). Essays are a great way to find out about writers.

NOTE TO SELF: Tell daughter to leave the twins in the cupboard and not be coming down around me, I'm reading essays today.

Pot Holes and a Gluten Free Donkey

Oh my God, I go to the Canary Islands for a week and what do I get when I come back? Nothing but scalding and unsettling news. Hasn't Galway County Council only gone back on a promise to give two million euro to the European City of Culture project. The promise was made last July when the announcement was made by the judges that Galway would be crowned Capital of Culture in 2020.

The same day the same people, the promisers were jumping and air punching and making unnatural screams on the street. Some would say howls of delight, others would say screams of embarrassment. The same day people were hugging on the street. Give me anything but air punching and pedestrian hugging.

Hugging is for the bedroom, streets are for eating pizza and drinking out of cans. Add back slapping to the hugging and you turn into Sleeveeen Mc Slaphole within the hour. Because of all that unnatural affection and buffoonery, promises were made, two million of them to be exact.

Well as the man said, flying rashers are soon forgotten. So the two million that was proffered on the day of jubilation is now pulled back and stuck up in the consciousness of a minor civil servant or cross-referenced on an old computer somewhere in a stuffy office in the bowels of the county council.

Some of the reasons for the dirty double cross were reasonable. Some would say it is no double cross at all but only a postponed decision to cough up to two mill. One councillor was worried because some communities don't even have a playground, and two million would buy a nice few swings and a couple of roundabouts. The roundabouts could have an Yves Saint Laurent attitude about them. A swing will always be a swing.

There was talk that the kids in the 'no playgrounds' area spent a good chunk of every day drawing on the back of the yellow wallpaper with permanent purple markers for stimulation. Well it beats doing wheelies up and down the spine of a three legged llama that escaped from Coole Park.

Another decent councillor found the two million hard to digest when we have potholes that would knobble a gluten free donkey or bring a plough horse with a rare form of dermatitis to his knees. If we filled in the potholes first, slapped up a few roundabouts and took the permanent markers off the kids and gave them back their cans. Wouldn't the wallpaper be in a far better state?

* * *

If that is not bad enough I met two women. Neither of them carrying two pints but both of them carrying opinions. The first woman had a frisson of indignation about the trains. She said, be afraid, be very afraid, if you get on the train at Athenry and you don't pay for your ticket. Even if it's a one-way eight-euro fare. You will be pursued through the courts, as was the case a few weeks ago.

Sixteen passengers were called but only four were chosen. It's up to Matlock now to find the 'no shows,' and the guy who owes the €36, and the student who owes the €19. It's Matlock's job to slap a bench warrant on them. It would be easier to slap a happy face on a blobfish or an elephant seal than slap a bench warrant on one of the 'no shows'.

Wouldn't all this pursuing through the courts and running the legs off Matlock with the bench warrants, cost a lot more than the piddling Euros owed? Surely there are admin costs and solicitor's costs and the devil knows what costs involved when the legal route is pursued? Could this be why Irish Rail is bleeding from the engine out?

Next thing you know Matlock will want a shoe grant for all the leather he is using trying to locate the 'no shows'. Some say they are up in Nelly's room behind the wallpaper. Before you know it Matlock No. 2 will want a grant for riding the clutch, while he leans out the window of his old Studebaker or his brother's Chevrolet Caprice.

As for the second woman! There was no second woman, only the first woman had a split personality and a train fixation. She loved films about trains and she would tell you so straight up. Among her favourites were *Bullet to Beijing*, *Doctor Zhivago*, *Murder on the Orient Express*, *Night Train to Venice* – but right now her absolute favourite was *The Taking of Pelham 123* with Denzel Washington and John Travolta.

She knew John Travolta was all badass in it but as she said herself, if you don't feel the blood coursing through your veins occasionally what's the point in living? She grew tired of the buzz from bingo twenty years ago. She said it let her down like a damp ham sandwich above at Knock Shrine.

She said Athenry station would need to mind itself or it could find itself like *Pelham 123*, getting hijacked by a gangster called Ryder. He'd drive that train straight through the aforementioned Capital of Culture and no leather grant would save Matlock from Ryder's abominable manners. Furthermore, it would take a lot more than two million to repair the old walls of Galway that date back to the 12th century after a conversation with a runaway train.

The Long Tired Memory

When Catherine Corless started her research in 2012 for a local journal, she was interested in finding out about the mother and baby home in Tuam. She knew that the home was run by the Bon Secours sisters previously and she also knew that the home was levelled in 1971. As a historian, she deals in facts. She resists all opportunities to exaggerate even the slightest detail. So if she tells you something, you will know that it carries no embellishments of any kind. She is a truth-seeker, first foremost and last. She is not a saint, because saints don't get migraine. She does not take kindly to anyone glorifying her. Her focus now is on helping the families of the Tuam mother and baby home. She does this quietly and without fuss. She wanted nothing in return. Her work is entirely unconditional.

In 1975 when two twelve-year-old lads were out playing and messing around they came across a concrete structure with the cover slab broken. It was an old septic tank that had been dried up and defunct since 1935. They looked through the broken slab and saw that it contained a lot of small skulls and bones piled on top of each other. They were very frightened and they ran off. Later the priest was called.

In the past we did look to the priest for answers. Over the past while, I am sensing a certain souring towards the power of the priest in Irish society. At this time, back in 1975, the priest still had a lot of power in towns and villages throughout Ireland. He came with his goblet of holy water and he blessed the spot where the boys saw the bones. The County Council were sent for and the covering up began. More concrete than before; this time the slab would not crack.

Fast forward forty years and see Catherine Corless getting ready to unravel one of the greatest injustices in Irish society. She talked to many local people and older people who would have had first-hand knowledge about the mother and baby home. The mother and baby home was originally a workhouse. Not all the locals in Tuam were happy about the research Catherine Corless was doing. Some people in the town today would prefer if it was never mentioned. There is a move-on attitude carried by many.

The 'no' answers started coming from the nuns themselves. No they did not have that file, they had given it away. The other file was gone too and all the files were gone. They were given by the nuns to the County Council. The county council had given the files to the Health Board. She knew from data that many of the mothers that went to Tuam mother and baby home came from Galway and Mayo.

She wanted to know the answer to one simple question and it is that question that fuelled her further research. If, as it was rumoured, a lot of babies had died in the mother and baby home, where were they buried? Locals mentioned a small plot in the corner. A plot which the locals tended to and they kept in pristine condition for many years.

She did discover that a health inspector visited the home and in his report he mentions the various diseases. He mentioned things like malnutrition and pot-bellied children and children with wizened limbs. The report cited gastroenteritis and as she found out from the death certs that many of these conditions were put down as causes of death in the children. The health inspector in his report sometimes blamed traveller children for bringing in diseases. It would appear the health inspector was in cahoots with the nuns when he was writing his reports.

Catherine Corless discovered by working with records linked to the St Mary's mother-and-baby home that many infants died in the home run by Bon Secours between 1925 and 1961. Now it was no longer hearsay, she would go a step further. She set about getting each of the children a death certificate. To enable her to establish the truth she paid four euro for each death cert, at a total cost to her of €3,184. Her research shows that 796 children, mostly infants, died there. She discovered there were no burial records for the children and that many of them were buried in an unofficial graveyard at the rear of the former home.

When she contacted the Church about the revelations that hundreds of children were buried but unnamed the Church did not want to know. Their response was 'you are seeing the past through the prism of the present'. She did not give up, all she wanted to do was have the names of the children mentioned on a plaque. She wanted them to be remembered.

The mothers in the home breastfed the children for a year when they could. If the mother did not have the one hundred pounds to pay to take the baby out, the baby was kept and the mother was shunted out quietly and quickly, in many cases never to see her infant again.

The children who survived went to school locally in the Mercy and the Presentation. The hope amongst many now is that the Bon Secours order will disband. They may have viewed the defunct septic tank as a burial place for the infants but they were keeping that a secret. It would be a small comfort to know that the babies were wrapped in a gauze or a swaddling cloth. The woman who fell into one of the chambers said that it looked like cider bottles wrapped in something.

Will we be any better people because of this revelation? I don't know the answer to that. We don't tend to change our lives by what we hear. Yes we are shocked and horrified but after a certain time don't we all go back to doing our normal stuff? I haven't heard a lot from Church leaders in the past days.

We need to talk about shame. It's the elephant in the room and we need to dismantle it. The Church too needs a bit of dismantling. Was there ever a time when it didn't despise women? It's a pity our mothers and grandmothers had such blind devotion to the Church. They got nothing for it only fear. To feel shame is one thing, to be shamed is another. It's archaic and carries with it a kind of crucifixion. The crucifixion of women. The State after all cosies up to the Church in its attempts to suppress women. The children of the mother and baby home who survived were stigmatised daily.

The Long-Tired Memory

The children of sin
march out again
from behind the ten-foot wall.
They march to school
that's a hob-nail rule.

The march of the hob-nail beat
can be heard in the street,
in the houses, in the memory.
In the long-tired memory.

No need for anyone to look out
they know that sound.
The hob-nail memory
makes a hob-nail pound.
Children are on the march
in their hob-nail boots.

They arrived ten minutes late ,
they leave ten minutes early.
If you were bold
you were threatened
with a seat by a 'home baby.'
A home alone baby,
a nobody home baby.

A 'home baby'
carried the sin of the mother.
The priest and nun always win
against the sexual sin.

When school is over
they marched back
in their hob-nailed-boots.

Five or six-year olds.
The children of sin
march home again.
They march in
behind the wall
the ten-foot wall.

The march of the hob-nail beat,
never fading in the street,
in the houses, in the memory.
In the long-tired memory.

Rat Running into Genesis

The second you put your snout into Genesis, you walk straight into the apple. What Jezebel had it? Eve. Who did she offer it to? Uncle Adam. So much depends on the apple and so much depends on bad old Eve for proffering it. I heard a talk on radio one time about malignant shame. It's like your common or garden shame but it has much more blush about it. It's a first cousin of a word that was drummed into us at school – *náire*. Tá náire orm. The literal translation from the Irish is, shame is on me.

Well shame was on me recently when I was caught by an unmarked garda car for rat running. It was on a Sunday morning, no cars around so I thought I'll chance it. Matlock was parked out of sight and he put the siren on and I was nailed. I stopped when it was safe for me to do so. All of a sudden I'm a model citizen full of consideration for other drivers. A few minutes before this I took a very dangerous right turn and I got caught. I felt immediate shame. I felt guilty and embarrassed. I knew I had done wrong and I was going to have to pay the penalty. That little right turn cost me €60 and a dirty mark on my licence. Matlock's pupils widened as I half-attempted small talk.

A fortnight ago I said that Galway was morphing into a police state. An article in the Galway Independent this week adds weight to that assertion. It states that a Labour councillor raised the issue of hair-braiders in the city at a recent Joint Policing Committee (that would be the Thought Police). He stated that he counted at least eight braiders on the streets of Galway. I think it should be knocked on the head, he said. His objection is not because they are not Irish but because anyone could follow the same trend and it would just clog up our streets.

I am fidgeting with a poem about shame that I started some time ago but never finished. I used to rent a cottage in Spiddal to try and get some work done. If anyone else said they had to rent a cottage to work I'd have called them bourgeois. While I was there I did get work done and sometimes I loved to sit at the kitchen table and look out and admire the pheasants. While I was there, an American student interviewed me as part of her thesis. Later I read from her bound copy: 'Ms. Higgins liked nothing better of an afternoon than to sit in her cottage and look out at the peasants.' It was signed off on by four academics from her university.

The poem has nothing to do with the student but I am reminded of her as it all happened around that time. Nor has it anything to do with Archbishop Eamon Martin, despite his chilling lack of understanding for women who have suffered unspeakable grief at losing children with Fatal Fetal Abnormality and other serious conditions. His butter-cupping, power-of-the-Church focus on women who might have to do that journey of shame, is ill-thought-out and callous. Where was Mother Church's moral outrage when eight hundred babies' remains were unearthed in a former unmarried mothers' home in Tuam? The days of Kissing Bishop Browne's ring and being fearful of Rev. John Charles McQuaid-types are over. Someone should tell him.

Shame

Who told you that you were naked?
GENESIS

A fox traipsed up the bóithrín
so laid back, so handsome.
Eye candy for the vixen,
vexation for the rat.

Nothing sly about him,
except the slope of his spine
had 'dodgy' written all over it.
You could say supine
but you'd be just name-calling.
He was now walking like a cheetah,
long Nijinsky steps.
Kind of odd for a fox to ballet.
He knew more than he was letting on.

Next I notice he's sporting a wolfish grin,
not like himself at all.
No way did a sheep's tank top
slide off his shoulder.

Up or down I wasn't giving him another minute.
As it was I was making a right peata out of him.
I reached for my camera,
he reddened and ran.

A Thousand
Buttonholes Today

I collected the post from the hall. As I was going through it I noticed an envelope addressed to me had nothing in it. I caught the postman before he got back into his van. Ring the depot, he said nicely. I'm always grateful for nicely. The man at the depot explained that forty items came in yesterday with no contents in them and sixty items came in the day before with no contents in them. I was flabbergasted bigly. Oh they're from the credit union he said. The man from the credit union was in here yesterday filling those empty envelopes. The man from the depot said that twenty-five thousand items were sent out from the credit union and some got posted without their contents. They may have only been annual reports, but still. Weird or what! I dreamt I got empty envelopes once and I looked it up and it said when you dream of empty envelopes someone is going to give you an elephant.

I have to go out now and get a toner for my printer. Helen Josephine on the phone quoted a small mortgage plus VAT price for the toner that is compatible with my printer. Have you any seconds? I asked. What are seconds? she said. So we went on like this. Helen Josephine on the phone found a cheaper toner down the back of a filing cabinet that is only half the price of the aforementioned. I'll go over straight away. I won't be there she said, I'm in head office but I'll have it couriered over.

I get to the shop. I pay for the toner. The box is bigger than my printer but that is probably bubblewrap or maybe she slipped in an extra toner because I'm so friendly today. I always thought toner was a little something you poured into a side door in your printer and you held a wet wipe like a china cup as you did it.

I'm excited at the prospect of doing something technical myself, like putting the toner in my printer without help. Given that I have a problem using the remote controls at home, this feels liberating to me.

On the way home I'll cross over and cut out all the traffic. I'll be home in jig time and the copies will be flying out like harpies straight out of Brexit. I'll get two thousand copies from this toner as opposed to 95 from that other unfaithful yoke that let me down mid stanza. In all of this I can't stop thinking about the poor corncrake if those harpies get him, but that's for another day. I love copies. Never mind this nonsense that your computer will store it for you, or all those USB sticks you have in every room will store things for you. I still love a copy. I'm like a civil servant in a Russian novel that way, I like to make four copies of everything.

The short cut is often the long way round in the end. I must have taken the first right turn instead of the second. This place has a pong of rust factory belt about it. I used to work in some of these factories. They have different names now because they sold out and set up in remote islands on the other side of the world, where they could get people to do the same job for a fraction of the price of a toner. That's what happens when the multinationals pulled out. It knocked the shine off the factories, now they look like some schools do during the holidays. They have echoes but precious little else and no amount of shortcuts will put life into them. An empty factory will always be an empty factory. We need to have more of a culture of looking after the worker. Lately the worker is viewed as the server or at times the waster. Let the waster pay is a new slogan on the lips of every corncrake sniffing harpy.

I'm saying to myself, the buckle factory was there and the shirt factory was there. In the buckle factory, we counted buckles all day that were called after German rivers. I was straight out of school and the factories held a great excitement for me. You'd be like a buffalo bursting through a wall with excitement listening to these country lads talking about their Red Cortinas and the Ranch House dancehall. 'If she's not red keep her in the shed.'

In the shirt factory I was a trainee cutter but I had bad judgment and no maths, and oftentimes I cut crooked. On Friday afternoons, we got to buy shirts that were imperfect. These might be from the stack I cut, who knows? You might get a lovely front and when you got home and took the packaging off you found the shirt had no back at all. They were airy shirts, I'll say that for them.

The manager said to me one day, You might try the computer factory, after all the cutting-room is no place for a girl with your brains. I begged to differ but he pulled a stiff upper lip. I did move on to the computer factory but not before I tried my hand in the nut and washer factory. All day long we parted the nuts and washers. I still get reunion reminders from the shirt factory. I don't give good reunion. Anyway, anyone who has ever worn one of the shirts I cut will remember me.

So I get home, two days later, and unwrap the toner, just the one. It looks like a spare part for a combine harvester. I yank out the old toner which is nothing like I imagined. It's a beast but nothing like the beast that has to go in. I try to put in the new one. It looks too big for this lilliputian letterbox space in my printer. Since the cold spell of late, the hatchet is back in vogue. I fetch it and rub some butter on it to aid the sliding in of the toner. I eventually get it in. It doesn't work, neither does my printer since the toner rose like a phoenix out of its spine.

Work On

Nostalgia takes me back –
the shirt factory toilet.

Where country girls met
and sucked cigarette ends on Monday mornings.

Sunday night was discussed, the Ranch House,
his acreage, physique and the make of his car.

Precisely they swayed to and fro,
tannoy blasted sweet lyrics, their hero.

Two jived to the beat, two killed the smoke
and seven sank further into hand-basins.

Boisterous laughter echoed and betrayed lost time.
'Back to work, girls,' Supervisor sang.

A thousand buttonholes today.
A thousand Ranch House fantasies the weekend.

Work On.

More Staffless Libraries Malarky

Staffless libraries was a pilot project back in 2014. Now it is been rolled out relentlessly to towns and cities all over the country. In its very haphazard philosophy (longer opening hours, opening anytime logic), it undermines library staff. The message it gives out loud and clear is, we don't need you. When library staff are being undermined, as they are by the threat of staffless libraries, it is very hard for them to function on a daily basis. A climate of fear exists amongst library staff who fear for their livelihood. Many have families and mortgages and this threat of staffless library is having a very negative impact on their daily lives.

If a fraction of the money that is being thrown at this scheme was given to librarians to invest in new books then communities would benefit. A library is at the centre of any community and it acts in ways we are not always mindful of. A functioning library, staffed by real people, is a valuable asset to any society.

Libraries are to be lauded for the way they help vulnerable people in our society. Staffless would quickly put an end to any sense of care for the individual. How does a person with disability feature in the minister's plan? How do children feature in this setup? What happens if a very aggressive person preys on a vulnerable man or woman late at night in a staffless library? The person being preyed upon has to then have the wherewithal to ring a number and wait for help from the Gardaí or in some instances wait for a security firm to arrive.

In my opinion staffless libraries do not enhance good reading habits. The librarian is being undervalued and so is the library service. Staffless libraries will lead to many library closures.

I despair at what is happening to our libraries services. The notion of staffless libraries is in fact a money squeezing gimmick that has little or nothing to do with community or care or humanity. I despair. It's a no brainer when you think of the cost involved creating these dystopian empty shells. They should have a sign outside staffless libraries, 'Enter this empty shell and confound your emptiness'.

* * *

Sometimes if I can't sleep I put on headphones and listen to the radio. I have no idea what it must be like to sleep rough. This night recently I heard a man talk about sleeping in doorways and how some places use sprinklers to make it impossible for anyone to spend the night there. He used the line 'in a goof from the cold' which I magpied.

He Sings Happy Songs

At three in the morning
in a goof from the cold
you try to feel your toes.
The voice in your head says,
where the fuck are my toes?

Rent freeze, toe freeze, heart scald.
More Joseph and Mary moments.
No room in this doorway love,
when is the baby due?
Try the side of the tattoo shop.
You and Mary might get lucky,
It's a good skipper if you get in
before the sprinklers come on.

The sprinklers come on
and drench your sleeping bag.
What fool said,
homelessness is a state of mind?
He thought he was a poet,
a fool poet I'd say.

The rent is too high –
try that doorway but mind the sprinklers
that's what I tell them.
They activate them several times a night.
You can dodge them if you never sleep
and you'll never sleep in Dante's doorway
looking for your toes,
not in a wet sleeping bag anyway.

Forget the one beds –
unless you rob a bank to pay the rent.
Ging-a-ling raises the rent
because he can and he will
and he'll do it again.
Ging-a-ling sings happy songs.

Rogue Thoughts
in Coole Park

We didn't celebrate our wedding anniversary this Christmas. I can't recall right now why we got married so near Christmas and on a Sunday. Maybe the priest would not marry us on Christmas Eve and the day before that just happened to fall on a Sunday. We were young; perhaps we thought we were special in some way. I have news for me. In nineteen seventy three we were just the far side of hippy and spliff-land was becoming as faded as a used teabag.

We went for a walk in Coole Park on the morning of New Year's Eve. We were marking something but we weren't sure what. It had rained heavily overnight and now the fallen leaves had made a slippery bronze coat for Coole. Leaves with shades of rust side-stepped themselves and fell face down. What we could see looked like a layered cake that had caved in.

I have no sense of direction, I get lost going to the hot press, so we chose the path that was already made. We would walk as far as the lake: a body of water is often enchanting and then at least you have reached some point that might in a casual way be a terminus of sorts. All told it was an easy not very talkative walk, you might call it laid back, a stroll even but the fact that we walked for two hours took the stroll out of it. At some unconscious level I might have viewed the walk as a way of celebrating our wedding anniversary, a walk through our years together, if that's not too much blather.

On the walk I didn't have to name anything. I was a tour guide once and I can be a Chatty Katty. Today I didn't feel the need to say much. A soft rain almost made it romantic, in a cows-and-sheep Ireland kind of way. Himself being fairly practical commented on how those fallen trees would keep us in firewood for a long time, if we had a long time. After a pause that was by no means unpleasant, he said, I'd say you'd hear a few interesting sounds here at night. I don't think he was suggesting that we come out here at night. It was just a rogue remark and there was a place for it today of all days, on the cusp of 2017.

We went on like this for another while. An adjective like blissful was swanning around in my head but I never let it out for fear of shattering the stillness. However I did risk all by asking him the best way to get to Loughrea. I had planned to visit my friend Mary Dempsey in the New Year. You can't mean that you don't know the way to Loughrea! Well, I said, with that new roundabout and the new road, I'd rather take the old road.

Someone is making life easier for you but you want the hard way. No, I said, I want the old way. I'm thinking for a bit about how odd I am but I am OK about my oddness. Still after a long minute that could easily have been five, I ask him, do you think I'm odd? Very, he said, and he didn't feel the need to add any more words to that sentence. We walked on like this for another while and we found the lake. It was overrated. We were out of the shelter of the trees, and the rain had no longer a soft-day-thank-God feel about it. We had everything in that path that brought us to the lake but we wanted more, and more let us down. More is for morons.

Still I felt the need to mention Yeats and the swans and the fact that he probably stood here and admired them. Fair play to him, he said. He was going to say something else just then, but he didn't. Today words could get lost, go astray, there was no need for accounting. I didn't ask him what he was going to say.

I've often found the way he holds a word back until the right time to be an act of wisdom more than anything. I babble for Ireland and I can hardly process what I'm saying half the times.

My thoughts strayed back to his remark about what it must be like out here at night. I was now having a few rogue thoughts of my own. I wondered if people came out here at night and went further into the forest and made the beast with two backs, long after the witching hour. A few thoughts about Lyme disease crossed my mind, but now was not the time for tick talk.

At times it felt we were outside of language. Words didn't matter here, nothing mattered. Ease was here in all its glory and grace too had its place. We didn't take the path less travelled, we took the well-worn path. It serves us well.

Coole I know is important for wetland birds (I was a tour guide once) I had hoped we would hear or see the whooper swans, but they fancy low tides. Today however the waters were high and rising.

Flying Rashers are Soon Forgotten

The fruits of the new City Development Plan (aka The Magna Carta of the Western World) come into action this week in Galway. The food ban is hereby lifted and from henceforth you are more likely to get your glasses smashed by the bun of a leftover burger, or a slap from a flying rasher on the main street in Galway than you are from an altercation outside a fast food joint in Eyre Square at two in the morning. In geographical terms the lifted ban now incorporates the stretch from Liam Mellows elbow across from Richardson's pub, right down to the King's Head at the bend of High Street.

Why because? I'll tell you why because! The chief executive's heartrate went into clickity-clack mode when he heard the councillors define 'takeaway'. The Chief Executive, who is himself a very cultured individual, does not want to see Galway becoming a Temple Bar or our main street looking like O'Connell Street after a dirty weekend. He sees in his crystal ball that Galway is a more suitable spot for higher order fashion, be the hookie. He further added, not in so many words, that all the rasher flying and took-away-take-away would give the future Capital of Culture a very jaded experience. It wasn't all Dublin-bashing. One Councillor (according to *The City Tribune*) said it would be wanton vandalism and open the floodgates and turn Galway into a Milton Keynes-type establishment. Well the majority of the Councillors voted for this food ban to be lifted so you may ask yourself WTF. I hope they get the two million to replace those wonky cobblestones on the main thoroughfare before the first Mars Bar gets deep fried.

* * *

Every now and then a true poet comes along. Galway sailor extraordinaire, Enda O'Coineen is such a person. Recently he was forced to pull out of his round the world yacht race because of a broken mast. He had visited my grandsons' school, Scoil Fhursa, a few months beforehand and spoke to the students. My grandson Oisín said Enda was great fun, he told them how he got thrown out of school. His team was also in the school and they were all happy people laughing a lot, according to Oisín.

We kept up the conversation about his sea travels. I can't know what the following hours and days were really like for him when that nasty gust broke his mast. Where did he draw strength from then? For what it's worth, his visit to Scoil Fhursa in Galway last Autumn made an indelible impression on one young boy's life and imagination and I'm sure on many others.

* * *

I have read the articles about nurses in Galway suffering from burnout. I was sorry to learn it but I was not surprised. Recently when my daughter Jennifer was in the maternity after the birth of her third son Jackson, most of the staff were helpful and kind to her, but a few were not. She was readmitted a few days after being discharged when some peculiar virus that was difficult to diagnose took hold of her.

While she was in the first time I noticed how differently some of the staff was treating a traveller woman in the same ward. When they addressed her their tone became high-pitched, indicating a little sneer. 'How are we today, how come we can't leave the cannula in our arm?' The traveller woman kept nipping out to the chapel and to have little bits of conversation with her other children on the phone. When she spoke on the phone every one of her comments to her children sang, it was all lullaby. The eight at home were missing her but she had some complications and had to stay longer.

I noticed in this six-bed ward all the women were after having C-sections and after the initial strong painkillers wore off the women were in agony. The patients one after the other were ringing for attention. To each patient the nurse distributing the medication would say, 'You are down for two Panadol and you will get two more in six hours.' What good would two Panadol do for a woman who just had major surgery? I wondered if this was some kind of judgment by the powers-that-be who disapproved of the C-section, which can be a life-saving operation in many pregnancies (as it was in my daughter's case). Was it because of cutbacks? Were they told not to distribute stronger painkillers that were more costly? The patients were puzzled and the visitors were puzzled. Women were leaving early so they could get stronger pain relief outside the hospital.

Fungus at the Back of My Fridge

I've been putting off cleaning the fungus from the back of the fridge for too long now. Today is going to be the day. I don't know why I put it off, it's not like I don't have a humdinger of an unused steamer just plonked there. The thoughts of taking out the inside trays from the fridge makes the job seem a bit laborious. They have to be washed separately, gawd the drudgery. Then finding bits of old shrivelled carrots that resemble the toes of the Tollund Man does not help either.

* * *

It hardly matters when you think of the two homeless people who were forced to sleep in the public toilets in Eyre Square recently. How could their basic needs not be met in a city where millions are being invested in propping up the Capital of Culture's gold laurel wreath?

We have a great little city here, *a pity little city, a shitty little city*. Some of the people who find themselves homeless in Galway are sleeping in doorways and car parks and church grounds. Only last week ten traveller families, nearly all with young children, were threatened with eviction from the Cúl Trá halting site. Land for that particular halting site was made available by the late Bishop Eamonn Casey.

* * *

My procrastination mostly figures around my own writing. I'll usually do something else, anything else, but it won't be cleaning the fridge. It will more likely be moving paper from one part of my box room to the other and praising myself into the bargain. There now, doesn't that look tidy? Paper pushing, I think it's called.

I need to be laughing while I'm cleaning the fridge otherwise I'll be crying. So I need to be thinking about some Bally-magash-ery I've read in my favourite local paper, the City Turbine. It never lets me down for cutting edge intel. Go on, Dara Bradley.

I'm thinking about a recent news item, whereby a salvo was fired by a former Fianna Fail Deputy Mayor. He opined with gusto that Pope Francis would bypass Galway during his visit to Ireland next year because the City Council had made a decision to stop the prayer before council meetings. I don't know what prayer they used to say; perhaps it was a rousing rendition of the Hail Holy Queen, a favourite prayer of mine as a child.

The Pontiff has so little for doing that he may well close down Vatican City and call all his cardinals and bishops by megaphone and tell them, we are having a conclave at half four, we need to talk about Galway. Yo, he might say, we can't set foot in Galway, because the atheists up in City Hall have stopped their heart-stopping rendition of the Hail Holy Queen, before meetings.

The decision to abandon the prayer before meetings was voted on earlier in the year. A majority voted against the prayer. The democratic decision does not seem to matter to the former Fianna Fail deputy mayor who says, 'The pope hasn't a notion of coming to Galway next year if this is the craic we're at.' Some councillors believe that in a rapidly changing Ireland we should maybe hold our whist before meetings.

I'm not a great one for prayer myself but I certainly can see how comforting it can be for people. Prayers should never be used as a threat. Prayer is a private thing between you and your conscience. I'm more of a wan for 'the aspirations' myself. When any of my grandchildren are sick, I say to myself, dear Jesus please mind that child and save him from all harm. That type of thing. I'm afraid of dogs and when I used to sell encyclopaedias years ago, when I had no scruples, and a dog would chase me, I was very addicted to 'the aspirations' then also.

I come from a religious background and like many others we said the rosary every night, on our knees leaning against the kitchen chairs. Dr. Noel Browne was always mentioned in the trimmings and the conversion of Russia for some reason and many other people who apparently needed our prayers.

* * *

It would be impossible not to have heard some mention of James Joyce over this past week. The way I see it, you are either a Solpadeine woman or a Nurofen Plus woman. You are either Yeatsian or Joycean. Personally I prefer Nurofen Plus and Joyce; he is that rare writer who voices what's going on in the mind before it reaches the tip of the tongue. He sifts after, we tend to sift before. We clean up, he cleans down, if at all.

He uses a mixture of styles, like parody, high-flown prose and internal, entertaining monologues. So if you miss him at one crossroads you'll catch up with him down the road. *Ulysses* can be as difficult as you make it or as enjoyable as you allow it to be. Let it wash over you and see how many Joycean gems you can catch with the magnet that is your imagination.

When Joyce's mother was dying, he was out of the country and he had to be sent for. His mother doted on him. On her deathbed she begged him to go to confession and receive Holy Communion. May Joyce died in 1903 and her final wish was not granted by her adored son, Sonny Jim as his father called him. Remorse figures bigly in *Ulysses*, as do the sins of the past. Joyce was not going to allow the overwhelming car crash effect of an event like the one at his mother's deathbed to pass him by. It would feature in many guises in *Ulysses*, not least with the religious term (he more than likely learned in Clongowes or Belvedere College) 'agenbite of inwit' which means 'remorse of conscience.'

The Power of Prayer

I liked the way
my mother
got off her bike
to the side
while the bike
was still moving,
graceful as a bird.
We watched out for her
after Benediction.
It was a game —
who saw her head-scarf first,
I nearly always won.
The day the youngest
drank paraffin oil
we didn't know what to do.
All goofed round the gable end,
we watched, we waited,
head-scarf over the hill.
Knowing there was something wrong
she threw the bike down
and ran.
She cleared fences
with the ailing child,
Mrs Burke gave a spoon of jam,
the child was saved.
Marched indoors
we feared the worst,
our mother knew
what the problem was.
'Not enough prayers
are being said in this house.'
While the paraffin child
bounced in her cot
we prayed and prayed.

We did the Creed,
a blast of the Beatitudes
the black fast was mentioned,
the Confiteor was said
like it was never said before,
Marie Goretti was called
so was Martha,
we climaxed on the Magnificat.
After that it was all personal stuff.
I liked the way
my mother
got off her bike
to the side
while the bike
was still moving,
graceful as a bird.
For good neighbours with jam
for pope's intentions
for God's holy will
for the something of saints
the forgiveness of sins
for the conversion of Russia
for Doctor Noel Browne
for the lads in the Congo
for everyone in Biafra
for Uncle Andy's crazy bowel
for ingrown toenails
and above all
for the grace of a happy death.

Cobblestone Currency

There is no poetic language, no euphemisms or no metaphors needed to describe the ongoing homelessness crisis on the streets of Galway. The timeline here is the fading days of 2016. This is the so-called arty city which will be lauded with the Capital of Culture crown in 2020. Two terrapin structures are being quickly assembled to accommodate the homeless on council property near the homeless day centre. Escalating rents, already overpriced, have contributed greatly to the homelessness problem here. Properties, including apartment blocks, are being bought up by the ghoulish, aptly-named vulture funds. Making the high rents impossible for many to afford, further stripping people of their dignity. These bone-picking developers are greatly contributing to Galway's homelessness crisis. Mental health is a factor in some cases, so is addiction.

* * *

A new phenomenon in Galway is the crooked cobblestones on the main shopping area. These cobbles have to be replaced at a cost of a mere two million euro, for crying out loud. This is nearly as much as it cost to lay down a bid to make Galway the Capital of Culture. Am I mistaken or have they not replaced these cobbles already? Just asking! The dig will not start just before Christmas as you might expect but the two million euro job will get cracking very early in the New Year.

The cobbles have to be changed and made smooth because people are nose-diving whilst looking for the subterranean passages that old Galway is better known for. Untold millions have been paid out in compensation already because of the haphazard nature of the ashen-coloured cobbles. Does no one inspect the work as it's being done? Surely that would save a lot of money! As it stands (no pun intended) some of the cobblestones resemble a chevaux-de-frise the likes of which you'd only see around a Norman castle to keep out bloodthirsty invaders with a penchant for pain but never a plenary indulgence.

* * *

Jackson Higgins, a brother to the twins Cooper and Axel, has arrived on Planet Earth. (The twins are 13 months old to the day.) We are overjoyed at the news of our new grandson, cousin to Oisín, my Pokémon-hunting partner and swimming buddy. It was a high-risk pregnancy for mother and baby. The twins were born with low platelets and they had to stay in intensive care for a few weeks when they arrived last year. Jackson's platelet count was just six and it should be somewhere between 200 and 250, so he will be in intensive care for a little while. He is wearing special glasses in the incubator because he is a little jaundiced. Jennifer, the baby's mother, had developed lupus during the pregnancy and a whole host of worrying things happened. The latest was a perforated eardrum just a few days before the birth. I asked Himself this morning over our porridge if he thought I was a worrier? He replied, the worst. Subject closed.

It was my good fortune to receive a Christmas card from a dear friend, Fr Pat O'Brien, from the parish of Carlistrane, this morning. I rang him, as his card arrived not long after the birth of our new grandson Jackson. I make connections when it suits me to do so and when I feel an overwhelming sense of something good in the ether. When happenstance is leading the charge or it seems so to you, you embrace that single positive frisson and you say yes to the power of whatever alchemy is at work to make good happen or seem to happen. It's enough for a doubter to believe for the blink of an eye. The currency of that blink can be stretched to infinity, with a little will.

Pat was getting off the train in Dublin when I rang; he was going to visit his aunt. I asked him at Jennifer's request if he would christen the three boys in April of next year. The twins are going around like two little Bally Bane pagans this past year. Well not after April, when Fr. Pat with one fell swoop will christen the three amigos.

We chatted briefly about the great loss of John Montague to literary Ireland and his many friends. I was asking Pat had he seen him in the Town Hall at Cúirt when he read with Paul Muldoon? He had, he said, and he had seen Seamus Heaney read there the year before them. In jest one of us said, maybe we should avoid the Town Hall for a while; in jest, the other agreed.

I'm rushing in to town now to have coffee with my friend Eva Bourke. We have been meeting for a long time. Since my own girls were born, since I wrote my first poem, since before the pope came to Bally Brit, since before the currency change.

The Minister, Dry Socket and the Novena

The minister was here and so was the novena. I have no way of knowing how long each will last in the memory. We forget pain, hard as that may be to believe but we forget pain. It lands and hides somewhere in the deep recesses of the mind. I had 'dry socket' once and it nearly did for me, the pain lasted for nearly three weeks. Dry socket happens when you don't do exactly what your dentist tells you to do after an extraction.

I swore I'd never forget the pain. Why would anyone want to remember pain and even swear to themselves that they would never forget it? I didn't remember the pain at all but I did remember the misery. We remember misery because sometimes we want to. We collect it and we store it in a safe box at the back of the mind and every now and then we drip feed it to ourselves and to those around us.

The minister for health was here and so was the novena. It's a no brainer to have the novena slap bang in the middle of Galway, where the streets are as narrow as they were in the sixteenth century. Guess what, we have just been lauded with another award. Galway has just been named the most congested city in Ireland. The survey was conducted by Inrix, a provider of traffic information worldwide.

Why don't they have the novena once or even twice a day in the racecourse instead of eight or nine times a day in a car-logged city. They could have a large tent or bespoke tarpaulins from Done Deal or Woodies at the racecourse to protect people from the elements. Free buses from Galway even but get that bloody novena out of the city for the love and honour of God. Do you know why I won't go to hell for saying that, because there is no hell! There is only traffic and a minister for health who bypassed us for months.

Should we now be grateful for his visit? A lot of patients who were awaiting discharge had to wait four to five hours until the minister had left the building. What good did it do to have the minister come to Galway? Should we have kowtowed in gratitude because the minister for health remembered that there is a place called Galway? Rag Week was on as well (although it was only on for seven days as opposed to nine days for the novena) so it was gawks-ville versus Jesus Loves You, and the minister has landed.

When you become invisible, you can see out but no one can see you. This is exactly what happened to a patient with stage four cancer during the week in UHG. He became invisible. He was too weak to walk to the toilet, so he asked for a bottle which was supplied to him. The only problem was that it was still there two days later full to overflowing. He asked me not to mention his name but he is a real person, this is not a 'I met a man with two pints' story. This is not a story, it is someone's reality.

When the minister came to the hospital there was a photoshoot to advertise Saolta's cancer care annual report. The minister didn't know about the invisible man with stage four cancer who was mortified someone would knock over the urine vessel that lay by his bed for two days. When the minister did speak he used a very knackered rhetoric like 'much-needed investment' and 'need to be looked at' and 'new A&E being designed' etc. We have heard all this before. It reminded me of Dante's quote: 'There is no greater sorrow than to recall happiness in times of misery.' He went on to tell us the waiting lists in Galway were some of the worst in the country. Ah hello, we knew that also. Internal hospital documents revealed that 2,500 patients waited over 24 hours to get treatment (City Tribune). That was in briefing material prepared for the Minister for his December visit that never happened.

In my opinion, his visit was a total waste of time. Why didn't he come unannounced? Instead his arrival was shouted from the rooftops. There was nothing but press releases and news items on local radio about his arrival. The whole schmaltz around the visit of the minister was reminiscent of a juvenile excitement at seeing new television programmes starting in the sixties like *Get Smart* or *The Virginian* or *Daniel Boone*. The city was flappin' with expectation, what we got was *Rowan and Martin's Laugh-In* or was it *Mr. Ed The Talking Horse*? As for it staying in the memory, I don't think so, the whole thing was eerily vacuous.

If he came unannounced and walked through the wards he would have got the real picture of a crumbling, overcrowded hospital. If he walked around St. Enda's ward, aka The Gulag or, as a woman who has just spent a week there called it, the last outpost, he would have got the real picture of mayhem. The first thing anyone will tell you in St. Enda's is 'don't touch the remote control, it's full of nasties.' Nasties that would kill Rin Tin Tin if he made an appearance. The hospital should be turned into a cats and dogs home because it is not fit for purpose.

It was all a step back in time or, put another way, a backward step. What we got was a staged version like you'd see in the movies when rich patrons came to view an orphanage. All the good toys and the sparkle was brought out. When the show was over the shabby was brought back and that aching gulf for change remained. What a wasted opportunity? I didn't see any nurses in the photoshoot, the ones keeping that hospital together.

You'd Feel Sorry for Peter
When the Cock Crew

My father used to say, 'don't smoke on the street and don't be caught dead in those shameful tight slacks'. The word *don't* had currency. It was delivered with rocks and chains. You knew the strength of it. *Don't* and you didn't until you got a little older, the voice in your head became stronger and said 'don't listen to don't listen to do and go and do.'

In William Trevor's short story 'Her Mother's Daughter' he opens with, 'Her mother considered it ill-bred to eat sweets on the street, and worse to eat fruit or ice cream.' Personally I don't like to see a person eating a bun on the street, a big cream bun. It's not the place for it somehow. Yet in London or New York, people walk faster and a lot of them are eating as they walk. The hurry brigade, they have a life and you are watching the world go by.

I dislike the London cafés where people stand up while they eat. What about the weight of their feet that we have been brainwashed with. Take the weight off your feet. Coffee to go is one thing but it seems all wrong to me to eat when you are standing up.

A few months ago I was invited to read in Ulverston in the UK. I noticed a woman on the train nursing a slice of cake in a see-through container. The cake looked like it was made from a charge of lemon lightness. The deliciousness of its look was magnified because it was somehow untouchable in its container. It rested on the table between us. I assumed she was bringing it home to have it with a cup of tea while she was watching her favourite TV programme. I felt like shouting, I'll give you ten pounds for it and a French kiss. The unsayable stayed where the unsayable stays.

I'm thinking about poems and short stories that have a powerful charge for me. One poem in particular by Martina Evans cracks me up. It's called 'Facing the Public, she recorded it at Kenny's and it's on YouTube. Her mother creeps into her poems a lot since she passed, says Martina. In the poem, Martina Evans flags the emphasis her mother puts on words. She says 'I'm asking you for the last time' or 'I'm imploring you,' or she says 'Never never never' would she be able to face the public again.

Like with William Trevor, we get it and we know what Evans means and it transports us to an Ireland that carried all the figaries and the dance that goes with them. When we identify with something in literature, we drag it along with us, it's not our own story but a gap between worlds where characters like those we read about can and do exist.

In the William Trevor story, 'Her Mother's Daughter' we meet one of the coldest and spikiest mothers. It's impossible to find something to like about her. He never wastes a word. The mother can deliver with a look what most writers need a paragraph for.

She is by all accounts a complex, unloving mother. Not all mothers are perfect. I could not identify with this mother in any shape or form. I loved reading the story and I was grateful to Trevor for creating it. It's a powerful story with a shattering ending that you happen upon in about five or six words. Evans' poem is equally powerful but you love the mother in it. You can hear and see her every quip. The poem and the story are in my head now. Evans' tone acts as a see-saw for us to balance the stunningly crafted vignette with. It could be a Fellini film.

* * *

I'm in Inverin this week housesitting. I'm dying to meet someone to speak Irish with but everyone is indoors hiding from me. I heard the cockerel a few mornings ago and I also heard the pheasant. The pheasant sound is not so pleasant. No rhyme intended. It's rusty and incongruous, for such a handsome bird.

Today I saw a male pheasant chase another pheasant around the garden; I presume it was a female. The male was colourful with his feathers all ruffled around his head. He scurried around the garden, his feathers fanning like a vampire's cloak over one pheasant eye, after the conservatively dressed female.

It must be their mating season and they are freaking out the cockerel that is protecting his patch. The cockerel is crowing at half three in the afternoon now. I'm trying to think of cockerel references in literature but my brain is not kicking in.

The only thing I know about cockerels is you don't hear them in the city and you have to trim their spurs from time to time. A pair of large dog nail clippers is recommended and a big file for the smooth finish. I'd fancy my job. The biblical reference we all know: and the second time the cock crew, Peter recalled the words that Jesus said to him, "before the cock crows twice you shall deny me thrice." When Peter thought of that he wept.

Jesus, I love the bible. I must do a course in bible study. Poor Peter was mortified when he was caught out. You'd feel for him really.

The Master Builder Gets a Tan

I wish I'd seen Ralph Fiennes acting in Ibsen's play *The Master Builder*. It has a self-tortured protagonist, Solness (which sounds like soulless) the master builder. He is jealous of his young ambitious rivals and he carries bucketloads of guilt. He wears hubris like tight-fitting ski pants. His downfall is that he takes on more than he is able for, and in dealing with others he never sees the plank in his own eye. It has several other layers. It's tough enough to read and I am struggling with it. Ibsen says in *The Master Builder*, 'It is the small losses in life that cut one to the heart.' I love it when someone creates a character like Solness. I'm already afraid but the fear is hurting me lovely.

* * *

Recently I was at the Áras to celebrate Bloomsday with many others at a garden party. A couple of days after that I rang eFlow, the barrier-free tolling system. I spoke to a very nice eFlow man who took my credit card number but would not give me his second name. I thought that was a bit odd but I am odd and if I don't pay eFlow I could end up like the man on the Joe Duffy show who owed thousands because his bill kept multiplying. Save me from the multiplier. Neither a lender nor a …

Then today I get an email telling me to register now for eFlow but don't reply to this email because no one will reply to you, Billy No Mates. So why have I to register again and give my details if I gave them already to the nice man who would not give me his surname. So I ring eFlow and an equally nice woman tells me I owe two euro and something but they won't take it out of my account until next month.

But if you register you can see the previously unseen. You can see where you have been and where you are going to. I'm all confused and I do exactly what she tells me. I am convinced that I am seriously missing out on a Mystic Meg experience here. I try to register so that I can see into oblivion. Like life isn't weird enough. Now with the help of eFlow I can see my journeys online. The journeys I take and the journeys I leave behind, the road less travelled.

Then I run out to see what my reg number is and I run in and add that and then I add another long number which is my account number and then I get an oops! I hate when I get an oops! It just means I have to keep running out to check my reg. number and start all over again. Then it seems a person with my email is already registered. Yeah that would be me. The man with no name who took my credit card details set me up that time, I'm thinking. Anyway I mostly get the bus and I rarely use eFlow, what am I worrying about? How often am I going to get an invite to the Áras? When we have a different president I'll never get to see the inside of the Áras again.

* * *

Well all that eFlow diversion got my mind off the very unnerving thoughts that a skyscraper is planned for Eyre Square East Quarter. Complete with hotel, shops, offices, apartments. That's not all, this is only a tiny part of a massive area of the city has been labelled a Designated Regeneration Area in the Developmental Plan. The areas in question are: the inner docks, Ceannt Station and the Headford Road developments. To me it all looks like a big business centre. Having an almost non-existent residential mix in these proposals is absolutely sacrilegious given the city's housing crisis.

However, there are plans for luxury student accommodation. I'd say by the time Mummy and Daddy are finished paying rent on these luxury apartments there will be very little in the kitty. Oddly in this so-called oasis of culture, a minuscule amount of cultural space is allotted, the irony of that! Some people from the arts world did object. Cúirt director and former Macnas director Padraic Breathnach said, 'In my view the cultural space allocation contravenes the spirit of the city plan.' Other objections to the plans for an urban quarter at Galway docks come from former Artistic Director of Galway Arts Festival Trish Forde, and Tom Conroy, who served on the board of Galway Arts Festival. Corporate bodies are delighted with the whole development plans.

Some people, myself included, feel it will destroy the medieval aspect of Galway. Only very recently after the concrete facade was removed from Garavan's pub, several intricate medieval carvings were revealed, giving us a glimpse of what a beautiful place Galway was in days gone by. Soon it will be little more than a facade if all these planned developments get oxygen.

Galway in the future will more likely resemble a mini New York but with little of the New York infrastructure. The buildings suggested in the developmental plan have hideous written all over them. Retired environmental editor of the *Irish Times* Frank McDonald described the proposed plans at Boham Quay (new docks) as 'ghastly generic anywhere stuff.'

Now most disturbing of all is that the council is not preparing any LAPs (local area plans), they are relying on developer-led plans, to save money, I suspect. Is this not a very dangerous route for the council to take, not to mention setting a very dangerous precedent? Does the planning department in Galway not remember the collapse of the Celtic Tiger? Did developers not strut around like Greek Gods, their LAPs in their togas, their heads in the clouds? As Ibsen said in *The Master Builder*, 'Castles in the air – they are so easy to take refuge in. And easy to build, too.'

Adding to the disturbing aspect of all of this is the fact that there is little or no public consultation about all these massive developments. I ask you, WTF is going on here?

Master Master, Where's the Plan?

When is a plan not a plan?
When there is no master plan.
When is a master plan
a framework plan?
Never.

The Master Builder gets a Tan
but he gets no master plan
There is no master-plan
there is no missus-plan,
there is only open plan
and knitting plan.
Knit me a building
and I'll wear it on my head
with a bronze tan plan
but no master-plan.

There are lap-dancers
and lap-lands
but no lap-plans
(local area plans)
there are lap-tops
belly tops, tank tops
developer-led plans
there is complan, rug-plan
a framework plan
but no master plan.

Give Me a Hundred, I Love the Parables

I feel awkward. I'd like to join a bible study group. What am I afraid of? Do I think that someone will slap me across the chops with Padre Pio's glove or sandal? No. It's not because I have fallen among thorns, even though I probably have fallen among thorns. I don't think I am having a crisis. I don't have time to have a crisis. No, it's much worse than that. I'm terrified that towards the end of the session I'd have to stand in a circle and hold hands with people I don't know. Albeit nice people who speak softly and I'm sure are very welcoming.

Give me a hundred, I love the parables. In the proverbs the fool gets an awful hammering. 'In the mouth of the fool is a rod for his back, but the lips of the wise preserve him.' *Proverbs 14.3.* I knew the Beatitudes by heart at one time. The Sermon on the Mount is another favourite. It's like magic realism in many ways. You can't quite believe it but you can use it as an analogy against today's awfulnesses. I'd like to think about the Bible the way I think and read great writers who give me a lot to think about. I want it to be a lens through which I can view the past and the present and I'm sure there will be similarities.

As Eliot said, 'There will be time, there will be time./To prepare a face to meet the faces that you meet.' I want to meet before the mask goes on, but no handholding or any other signs of intimacy.

* * *

Words matter, words don't matter. I like to look up words in actual dictionaries. I like hunting for a word. I have a Dineen Irish-English dictionary that I treasure. It was compiled by Fr. Patrick Dineen in 1927. I always wanted to dream in Irish and I want to have sex in Irish and no I don't want to film it. Dineen gives us a few great words for kiss in Irish. *Smaiseog* (a loud kiss); *Flaspóg* (an audible kiss); *Siosóg* (a sucking kiss); and *Póigín* (a little kiss); *Clapóg* and *Spailp* also mean kiss, according to Dineen. The University of Limerick have recently put Dineen's dictionary online. The only Irish word for kiss I knew before looking it up, was *póg*.

If a word has a biblical whiff off it I'd like to know where did it feature in the Bible. Take for example the word *trespass*. It's a word that got into my consciousness recently. It's hanging around like a corner boy in there and I can't seem to kick it to touch. When I think of *trespass* I think of childish images of orchard and apple and don't steal. As a woman, the apple will always be there to haunt you. What if Adam offered you the apple, would the balance of power as we know it be any different? Other ways *trespass* infiltrates this tiny mind is in relation to property. Along with property and trespass in my mind, comes a Keep Out sign in big bold print.

* * *

Residents of a leafy suburb in Galway are apoplectic with rage at Galway City Council's decision to include in the developmental plan the opening of a mosque in someone's house in Mincloon, by Jove. They want to change the use of a house to a place of worship. There are no limitations as to what this could mean, said the director of services at Galway City Council. According to *The City Tribune* one irate resident said the issue has nothing to do with multiculturalism, it's all about safe planning and safe roads and protecting all of the people of Galway and not just some of the people. Now that all reminds me of a relatively new word in the lexicon, *Rahoonery*, which gave rise to an anti-traveller sentiment in Rahoon when residents back in 1969 tried to remove travellers from their campsite by force. In the dictionary, *Rahoonery* is described as: noun (Ireland) — Violent anti-traveller sentiment and action.

The magic realism continued in the courts in Galway this week when a man was found brawling. Not the end of the world in itself but he was packin' a claw hammer in his underpants. He didn't have it there to tickle his cranium your honour. He had it there to pull teeth from his arse.

Recently the HSE has nobbled a memo which describes patients who overstay their welcome in hospital beds as trespassers. The inhumane memo stated that staff is legally entitled to remove the person (i.e. the eighty- or ninety-year-old patient) as a trespasser, using only minimum force, of course. What is minimum force when it's at home?

They Trespass Against Us

The memo said,
get them out of that bed,
make Lazarus out of the lot of them.
By the head or the knee,
a puck in the back,
a knuckle in the nuts,
but no head butts,
a sweeping ankle throw,
but no bruises.
They trespass against us.

Minimum force at all times,
except at tea times,
give them little, no tea, no ham,
give them spam.
They trespass against us.

Unwilling or unable
make them bed blockers stable.
Fed or unfed get them out of that bed,
but no bruises. Infirm or inform,
who cares if they're warm?
They trespass against us.

The Memo was meant
for senior management eyes only.
Written by their legal team,
paid to be mean, paid but not seen.
They trespass against us.

No One Mentioned
the Roofer

Last week when I was on my way to Ledbury in Herefordshire to give a reading, the news filtered through that my son-in-law Pat Mackey was taken to hospital by ambulance at 7.30 that morning. The news disturbed me a lot. Pat is forty five years old and he has terminal cancer. Normally some of the brilliant and kind palliative care team come to his house and give him pain relief and help him overcome bouts of nausea. So I'm thinking that he must be really much worse if he has to go to the hospital this morning.

Should I turn back? I haven't boarded my flight yet, I still have time to email the UK festival and cancel. I was advised not to cancel, that everything was going to be alright. Pat was now in Galway's accident and emergency department and he would soon be seen to. Or as they say in Connemara, *Ní mar a shíltear a bhítear,* things are never as they seem.

When I got home from Ledbury, which is a beautiful market town three trains and a shuttle away from Birmingham airport, I learned a few things about Pat's time in Galway's A&E department. Firstly he was half the day on the trolley in a very busy corridor before being moved to a cubicle. He was admitted by ambulance because of severe pain and an overwhelming feeling of weakness all over.

A nurse in A&E asked his wife, my daughter Heather, if she could find him some pain relief as they were not in a position to give him as much as a Dispirin until he was seen by one of the doctors from oncology. Heather went out and got over-the-counter painkillers from the chemist shop across the road. Finally, after waiting twelve hours in A&E Pat got a bed in St Enda's Ward.

There is a beautiful new oncology ward in Galway but Pat could not get in there yet. The hope was that he would be transferred there as an in-house chemo patient but if he goes home now he will miss his place and have to wait six weeks to get into this oncology suite. So St. Enda's it is, a long ward with an even longer history. I referred to it in a previous column as The Gulag.

This ward is truly abysmal. It is a general medical ward like the rest but this one in particular is used for psychiatric patients who are sent over from the psych ward. They have medical issues as well as mental health issues. That has nothing to do with its being abysmal. The men have to use the women's showers in St Enda's because the men's shower is used as a storeroom. So, very often as a woman is coming out of the shower a man is going in.

Some of the patients here from the psychiatric unit have one-to-one security guards sitting beside their beds. It is more reminiscent of a scene from Chekhov's *Ward No 6* than a scene from a hospital ward in 2017. It's survival of the fittest in St Enda's ward and, if you have stage four cancer like Pat does, and you don't sit up quickly and eat your dinner when it arrives, another patient will rock up and eat it without your permission, in jig time. The practice of other people eating your food also applied when my husband was in St Enda's in 2010. A confused patient often tried to get into his bed. You sleep with one eye open in St Enda's ward or not at all.

Another day Pat was feeling particularly unwell. Heather had to keep changing his t-shirt as he was perspiring profusely. He could have had an infection, he could have had sepsis, and there was no one to help him but his wife. Yet when she was coming back in after collecting her son the staff nurse said it is not visiting time. You can only come in here during visiting time. The same day a blood test was requested at 9.40am. That blood test didn't happen until 7pm.

Today Pat was seven days in St Enda's with no privacy and living in absolute fear with security guards sitting around the place. He could take it no longer; he was very distressed as there was no sign that he was going to be moved to oncology. He was given a calendar year to live last November by his oncologist. Pat is dying. When my daughter called up to him today after collecting their son Oisin, Pat had his few things packed and said that he wasn't being looked after and he wanted to go home.

In Galway's so-called cancer Centre of Excellence a dying man became invisible. He had no relative, surgeon or doctor who might get him into oncology a little quicker. He became like the character in Kafka's short story *A Hunger Artist*, who was just swept out with the straw from the cage in the end. He was invisible and unimportant, nobody cared.

As they were on the way home a nurse from bed management rang. Heather wanted to know why after a week Pat was still in this ward instead of the oncology ward and the nurse's exact words were, 'He just wasn't a priority.' He is at home now, hurt, dejected and feeling completely let down by the so-called cancer Centre of Excellence. Pat left school early and through an access course did a science degree in NUIG. He excelled with eight straight As. Before that he was a roofer.

No One Mentioned the Roofer

(for Pat Mackey)

We met the Minister,
we gave him buns, we admired his suit.
The band played, we all clapped.

No one mentioned the roofer;
whose overtime was cut
whose under time was cut
whose fringe was cut
whose shoelaces were cut
whose job was lost.

We searched for his job
but it had disappeared.
One of us should have said
to the Minister,

Hey Minister, we like your suit
have a bun, where are our jobs?
But there was no point;
he was here on a bun-eating session
not a job-finding session.

His hands were tied.
His tongue a marshmallow.

Calamus, Hyssop and Juniper

Developers don't tend to sit in a corner bathing their wounds with calamus, hyssop, and juniper. Not in Galway anyway. In a hoggish attempt at gentrification, two developers who own considerable property nearby are planning to make smithereens out of St Patrick's new church, and rebuild it elsewhere. It's like the scene from *Bugsy* when Warren Beatty walks into this house he wants with a suitcase full of money and says to the owner, sling your hook. The scope of the development if it goes ahead has that type of swagger about it. The buzzwords to note in the Developmental Plan are 'key opportunity site' and 'Eyre Square East Quarter.' The developers say the church would have to be rehoused. Otherwise where would they put their planned hotel, shops and apartments for the love and honour of Mike? So to be perfectly clear, they demolish and rebuild. *The City Tribune* features the story on its front page and rightly so.

Maybe the demolition of the church is indicative of what lies ahead, or at least it could be a muddled-up metaphor for our crashing times. Ten years ago at a funeral, I would not have placed a memorial card from Spar in the basket at the end of the coffin of someone I knew to have been a mass-goer. I would have been mortified and I'd have gone to great lengths to get that card signed by a priest. Even if it meant climbing up the side gable of a church that has not yet been dismantled and moved elsewhere. *Ireland is Changing Mother, tell yourself, tell your sons.* The Church is moving away from us or are we moving away from the church? Up or down it's cold up here on that gable-end, my nails hurt and my toes have frostbite. My back has Pilgrim's Progress emblazoned all over it.

* * *

The Church's response to the revelations by Catherine Corless, as heard on an RTE news report in 2014 was, 'We can't be looking at the past with today's vision' and oh yes we are still talking about the church. As for the past, as William Faulkner put it, 'The past is not dead it is not even past.' Speaking of the recent past that I hope we never look at with today's vision was another vigil. This time to mark the fourth anniversary of the death of Savita Halappanavar in Galway. It was graceful and powerful, and it was enhanced by the poetry of Elaine Feeney.

When Savita Halappanavar was begging for a termination in the maternity ward in Galway, none of us out there could help her. A medically trained person herself, she knew there was something drastically wrong, she had severe back pain and she was miscarrying. Although it was known at this stage that the pregnancy was not viable, Savita Halappanavar died of sepsis and multiple organ failure.

This was no unfortunate accident, not even an isolated incident. It was made possible by the 8th amendment, which is a profoundly disturbing piece of legislation with a deep disregard for women's lives. Because there was a foetal heartbeat, it did not matter how loud she cried or how long she begged for a termination, it was not going to happen because of the strictures of the 8th amendment. The foetal heartbeat had the same value as Savita Halappanavar's life.

It is additionally outrageous that women are accused of murder in relation to ending a pregnancy that is impossible for them to go ahead with, be it for medical or emotional grounds. It is an affront to suggest that this implies they do not love children. A mother and grandmother myself, I know the immense joy children bring to my life. But I would never wish the fate of Savita, and the many others who she represents, on any woman in Ireland.

* * *

Savage Grace is the name given to the Macnas parade this year. It displayed a meandering waltz between love and loss through the streets of Galway. I had a great vantage point from the back of an American-style pickup truck, that my grandson Oisín and I jumped up on. We were right at the back of the Courthouse and we saw love and loss crawling down the Salmon Weir Bridge. Thank you to whoever owns the truck and sorry for not asking permission. The parade had a giant owl, ravens, witches and wolves and we were mesmerised by the whole display. Fair play to the director, Noeline Kavanagh, for tapping into the child's and adult's imagination once again. She's a national treasure, that one. This is the kind of culture I love, the all-inclusive kind.

On the way home we had a slight altercation with two gardaí. They were standing so close together that you could not fit a slither of grease proof paper between them. The traffic was heavy as you can imagine. The town was emptying out after the parade. Matlock One waved us on. Matlock Two ran after us with a red sword-like thing that looks like it came straight out of *The Force Awakens*. He said you have to give way. My daughter Heather sitting beside me released the Kraken, and I am lucky to be here to write this instead of being shipped off to some unnameable dynasty as an indentured servant.

Like most writers I'm always on the lookout for new words. I heard a woman on radio recently talking about Hauling the Pulk. I didn't know what it meant but it sounded like something filthy you'd do with your significant other of an idle Sunday afternoon instead of reading the Life section of the Sunday Indo. I'll get Hauling the Pulk into a poem yet if it kills me, Mackenzie.

It Suits A Narrative

The other day I tuned in to the national radio station in the afternoon and I started picking up on a conversation mid-sentence. I'll stay listening, I thought, but I didn't know for certain what was going on. I knew it had something to do with the redress board Caranua – and it seemed so far-fetched I could hardly believe what I was hearing.

I had read an article in the paper earlier in the day and it was about people being unhappy about contacting the redress group.

I kept listening and tried to recall the newspaper article. People were ringing in and voicing how they were humiliated by the body that was supposed to be there to help them. A man said how he applied for money to do a counselling course so that he could get off the dole and help other people through counselling.

He was denied the money for the course, even though he had applied several times. He was over the limit because he had already received a couch and new windows. I remember Nelson Mandela saying: 'Education is the most powerful weapon which you can use to change the world.'

No money was given directly to the survivor from the redress board. The money was given directly to the carpenter or the undertaker or the educator. I stayed tuned in to the radio and heard a woman from the redress board saying 'it suits a narrative' – and then the article kind of came back to me. Or at least those words did: 'It suits a narrative.'

When I read it, I asked myself what that line meant: 'It suits a narrative.'

I kept listening to the radio programme. The attitude of the woman from Caranua (the redress board) was odd. She seemed impatient. She kept saying, 'No I didn't think we needed to ask for more money. I don't think more money would help.' She mentioned 'these people' a few times – 'these people, these people...'

She was referring to the people who were seeking assistance from the redress board, the people who had been in industrial schools and other Church-run institutions.

They never lost their identities but their identities were taken from them. Most people were given other people's names, other people's clothes, and other people abused them. There was no need to copperfasten this fact. After all, words matter. Words hurt. These people are the survivors of years of abuse by State-run organisations, and I thought they deserved better.

Not being listened to, and calls and emails not replied to, featured in loads of their grievances. Callers were frustrated and unable to cope with their frustration about being left hanging on the line by the redress staff.

Survivors of abuse should not be faced down by an organisation set up to help them. The vital ingredient of compassion appeared to be absent from the organisation's responses to the callers.

If a caller said, 'I was asked what institution I was in,' they were told: 'We never ask anyone what institution they were in.' It went on like this for a disturbing hour or so. The Caranua chief executive chided them for taking it to the media – but it all stemmed from her article in the paper earlier that day. It was she who had brought it media-side full and centre.

It was frightening to hear a helping organisation seem to belittle the callers – despite the fact that they were all survivors of childhood industrial school abuse.

Yes, survivors can be awkward, irritable, aggressive – but so what? They have been treated like sub-humans and they did not come out of it unscathed. We need a nurturing, kind, sympathetic person at the helm of any organisation who is dealing with people who have had their lives destroyed by abuse.

The machinations of the helping group need to be looked at – and the CEO needs to perhaps allow someone with a more relaxed disposition to talk to the survivors. At times like this a condescending and defensive attitude could be seen as teetering on contempt and arrogance.

It Suits a Narrative

Some applicants will never be happy
and grievances suit a narrative,
of the big bad Church
and the big bad State
and the big bad building
with the big bad gate.

We ration our compassion,
while all ye say suits a narrative
of the big bad State.

We ration our compassion
but we'll give you a couch.
We ration our compassion
but we'll give you new windows.

We are the keepers
of the Church's money
we divvy it out in dribs and drabs.
We won't give you money
but we'll give you new teeth,
a new radiator,
a brand new funeral.

It's not that we want your pain
to be everlasting,
but by the same token
it suits a narrative
for ye to come on here and complain

and say we have no compassion.

We have oodles of it,
but we ration our compassion.
If we give you stuff without humiliating
you
it won't feel right.
You ask, we give, or maybe we won't.

So fill that form and then fill another
and another and another
and one for your sister
and one for your brother
and while you're at it
one for your mother.

Don't listen to the guy who said,
criminal records are given out
like holy communion
to people in institutions.
We all know he stole an apple
otherwise why would he have been there?

Some applicants will never be happy
and it suits a narrative,
of the big bad church
and the big bad state
and the big bad building
with the big bad gate.

No One Ever Kisses You

It was a teenage wedding and the old folks wished them well. That's the opening line to the Chuck Berry song that John Travolta and Uma Thurman get up and dance to in *Pulp Fiction*. 'Don't you hate comfortable silences?' she says. Personally I don't mind silences, although Tarantino was trying to subvert the line by making Uma Thurman say comfortable silences rather than what might tumble off the tongue naturally, which would be uncomfortable silences. I believe a healthy silence always says something. It has no turns going on, no crossroads, no road signs, no bollards. It's just a wide open *Thelma and Louise* road or better still a Beckett road.

It's the quality of that silence that speaks. When you love someone, no interpretation is required for the silence that often happens organically. In fact that silence can be arousing if the eyes have a cameo part in it. In friendship too that silence can be like a slice of almond and lemon meringue. No one gets a bite but everyone gets a taste. It's the taste that matters. When you really dislike someone the silence can be poisonous. When two people have the poisonous silence, malevolence, spite and evil are never far away. You don't want that in your living room.

The awkward silence is the silence you created when you asked a woman how many months she was pregnant when in fact she wasn't pregnant at all. Lesson learned but you take responsibility for your own stupidity.

Or the mis-sent text. This guy sent me a text about me that he meant to send to his colleague. He said, 'Don't worry about her, she is a right prima donna.' He later asked me to write a blurb for his poetry collection. I explained to him how busy I was working on my prima-donna-ship.

* * *

I hadn't met The Chameleon (aka Lizard lips) and Lacuna on Mainguard Street for ages. I asked him if he was coming down from something as he was all Shakin' Stevens? I'm coming down from the attic in my mother's house, he said. We had to give up our flat because we got knocked off the sick. They were banging on about privatisation of the dole and Thatcherism and a litany of other stuff. They were dancing in the street to their own inner beat. You might rattle out a poem, he said. I'll try I said but I never know. Things are bad. Yeats's beast is slouching around Augustinian Street. Try harder.

* * *

A British firm called Seetec has won the contract to put smacht on people on the dole. It's bounty hunting by any other name. They are actively recruiting staff in the west for this humiliating drum roll.

When compassion is taken out of the equation a dehumanising element creeps in. The person asking the questions knows that they will get paid if they get you knocked off the sick. Pay by result, hello. It's called privatisation. We have been Seetecked. It's called Thatcherism and it's live and kicking in Galway and in Ireland in general. The system has already dehumanised the person asking the questions and they in turn are brainwashed by the Pay by Result mantra that is piped into their middle ear by their recruiters. If you don't get that guy in the wheelchair off disability you don't get paid, so ask him when his disability is going to clear up. Taking a person's dignity is inbuilt in any pay by result scheme. Your bosses will never be responsible because they didn't tell you to openly humiliate, but the whip hand for your wage packet did (i.e. pay by result).

No One Ever Kisses You

The contract was won
by a firm from across the pond.
They bounty hunt the sickly
and get them off the sick.
The shtick they use
is the tick-boxer.
They tick and they lock,
eyeball to eyeball.
It's like speed dating
only no one ever kisses you.
The answers must be wrong
cos they keep saying, wrong answer.
About your schizophrenic episodes
how long more are they going to last?
I don't know, I have no control over them.
Sorry, that's the wrong answer.
This Pay by Result scheme is mean. Next.
When is your disability going to clear up?
Wrong answer. Next.
Could you buff the blades
of an electric lawn mower
while it is still in motion?
Ah no, I don't think so.
That's the wrong answer.
You are hereby off the sick.
Don't bother ringing your doctor,
we've already been there done that.
We get paid by result
you gave the wrong answer,
close the door on your way out.

The Benevolent Coat Saver in Black

We get attached to coats and things. Once on my way to America I must have left my coat on the flight. I hadn't noticed until I got to my accommodation and not even then but when I went to go out. It was freezing so I had no option but to go into the first shop I saw and buy a coat. I bought a very light puffa type coat. I loved the coat because it was so light and so warm, it was so soft it could double as a pillow and I knew it would come in very handy leaning against that cold window on the Go Bus when I was heading back to Galway. When the coat was rolled up you slid it into this pouch and that was your roll pillow.

I was always boasting about the coat. People would say, are you not freezing in that light coat. Then I would launch into a big boast. The last time I boasted about it was to Gerald and Dorothea Dawe at a Yeats thing in The National Concert Hall some months back. They were well impressed, I could tell.

The next day I either left it in the back of a taxi or on a seat in Heuston Station when I bent down to tie the lace on my sneaker. I don't tie a good knot and I spent a lot of my life buckled over making the effort. I never get any better at tying shoelaces but I won't let it defeat me.

Recently I did a reading at Thoor Ballylee, aka Yeats Tower. I was reading with Jennifer Johnston. I inherit a lot of Lelia Doolan's friends as I have no friends of my own. I have been meeting Jennifer on and off for years and getting to know her bit by bit on every encounter. Nearly all our encounters are Lelia-linked.

I didn't expect any money for this gig at Thoor Ballylee because it was a fundraiser. Lelia, who organised the reading, stuffed something into my pocket. This happened as I was leaving her cottage hours after the event. Six of us were after having a lovely meal of lamb curry on a bed of mashed potato and cabbage. It was delicious. Maureen Clancy brought dessert, caramelised pineapple slices dusted with cinnamon. You could further embellish the dessert with yoghurt and/or cream.

It might surprise some to know that I am not a great mixer and this is about the second dinner thing I was at in my whole life. I really enjoyed it. My social life is me going to the pictures on my own. I always buy a packet of M&Ms and a cup of tea and I am the happiest person in the cinema.

Because I got money I was not expecting for the reading I said to myself I'll buy myself a jacket in TK Maxx. I did. A lovely light purple one. I call it The Tower Jacket. I love it .It's turned into my second skin. I'm so afraid I'll lose it I wear it in bed with the runners himself put a good knot in. A knot that will keep. I had another lovely black and white coat years ago when I sold encyclopaedias. I lost that as well. I still think of it. I was seventeen when I lost that coat. It was lovely on me but not so comfortable. Nowadays I go in more for creature comforts, the pillow for leaning against the bus window.

I worked in a secondhand clothes shop once, it was a few shops away from Kenny's Bookshop on Quay Street. It was called Second Hand, oddly enough. We sold a lot of coats. Later when I started to write, I wrote a poem called "The Benevolent Coat Saver in Black" about a memory relating to the shop.

I can rattle off the small losses and there were many. The bigger losses are harder to nail down. They queue jump and they chime at the back of the throat. They rarely reach whisper. They never reach howl.

The Benevolent
Coat Saver in Black

(for Angela Small)

In the doorway of our shop this ebon nun
declared it, 'Something to save my good coat'.

'The size doesn't matter but the colour, yes,
it must be a dark shade of black.

This seems adequate, but yellow,
it won't match the colour of my faith.

My faith is black as black as a crow,
I'm saving my good coat. Did I mention?

This, a bit smockish, too wide,
much room for secrets, not allowed'

'It suits you grand,
blends in darkly with your glance.

It's yours for a prayer, will you have it?'
'No it's the wrong colour black.'

'You have a merciful back to save your good coat,
will you save mine as well?'

from *Goddess on the Mervue Bus* (Salmon Poetry 1986)

Shoe Box, Man Shed, Silverback

I've often heard that water and fish create good karma around the house, inside and out. For many years we have had a water feature that trickles down onto a man-made large fish tank or fish hole or fish house, whatever you would like to call it. I'd say fish pond but that gives it rather a nice look whereas it has far more character than a mere pond but I can't find the word to best describe it. Himself made it one afternoon and over time he added some lovely looking fish, none of them any bigger than a fat trout but all of them bigger than a goldfish. When the estate is quiet at night you can hear the water trickle down, creating a comfortable sound that echoes and repeats. The rippling never stops unless we have a power cut. The water comes from a rain barrel outside the back door and the pipes or tubes that carry it to little Niagara are concealed in the earth. The motor is, of course, powered by electricity. No matter what country I am in I am always happiest to hear this sound. I'm home. This morning when I was putting on the kettle I noticed something colourful on the path halfway up to the man shed. I thought first it was sweet wrappers. When I investigated further I discovered that one of the bigger fish, not quite like a fat trout but so so, had gotten out of the fish tank thing. His head and eyes were visible and his lower body was eaten. I called himself in a panic; one of your lovely fish is dead. Don't tell me it's the lovely red one, he said. No, I said, it's the lovely orange one. I don't have an orange one, he said. It wasn't the time to argue the toss on the hue of the half-eaten fish. I said orange is the new red, that got no laughs at all. If ever he happened to be away without me he would always say, don't forget to feed the fish and let the rainwater drain off into so-called pond. I overfed the silverback and he died. He was a greedy fish and always jumped up showing off and grabbing the fish feed before any of the smaller fish had a chance. I buried him in a shoebox in the garden. My grandson was there and I thought it would be like I was throwing him a Grizzly Adams-type learning adventure. Fish dies, bury fish type of lesson. It actually traumatised my grandson who, ever since, won't go to movies with fish in them. He has to wait outside the cinema while I watch *Finding Nemo*, A *Shark Tale* and *Finding Dory*. I don't know how to identify a fish's gender so I call them all he. The only thing we know for certain is that when a bomb is being dropped in Afghanistan it's a she, it's called the mother of all bombs. In Venezuela the protest set for this week is called the mother of all protests. Are we becoming more powerful in the face of war and protest or is it just macho shite talk? Sometimes men call engines 'she' — *'she's after collapsing on me again, she is the bitch.'* I never told himself about the silverback; he thinks a hawk might have taken it but I did mention hawks don't like the estate; too many council houses and piebalds.

II

Manifesto for Poetry

A poem does not have to be nice. I want a poem to make me think or feel something about someone, some place or thing I didn't know about. If the poem makes me feel about it in a different way, I consider that a bonus. I don't have to be able to relate to the poem, but if I can, that always helps. I remember a poem that I can enter into imaginatively much longer than I remember a rattle bag of abstractions.

If a poem can make you feel the truth of it, regardless of how the poet came to that truth, it adds to the currency of that poem. Yes, poems have value and so do poets. Conversational poems have as much value to me as the well-wrought Alexandrine.

For me a poem should have an inner dance. I'm not suggesting a cross between a Highland Fling and Riverdance, something a bit more subtle than that. A YOU rhythm. It's yours and it relates to the poem that you are working on. You hear it in the ear first and then you internalise it and you tap away and let each word fall against the next word. If it's a wrong sound your inbuilt rhythm detector will know and then you start rewriting. If the music is cut, the dance is also cut. Too much punctuation can play puck with your inner dance. In my first collection I had very little punctuation that was not suggested to me by helpful editors. Less is still more to me in terms of punctuation, but I do understand that a poem has to be sort of comprehensible to anyone who may read it.

Tone is important too; it is a window into the writer's view of their subject, whether they are laughing or crying, or both, whether they are saying one thing and meaning another. There is room for that too. There is room for the slip sliding of the language that is there to be played with, to be sung, to be flogged, to be robbed. Take a word, any word, it's now yours, do what you like with it. Nowhere is there such freedom.

Something has to happen to herald the start of a poem for me, like a sound, or a song on the radio, or a dream, or a smell from childhood. I would not call this thing that happens mysterious but it certainly is unpredictable. It could be a ping or it could be a shiver.

And occasionally, the call is different altogether: Galway in the west of Ireland where I was born, was bidding to become The European Capital of Culture in 2020. I was asked to meet some members of the 2020 committee over lunch to discuss a project. The bid, I was informed, represented an opportunity for us to come together as a community, to reflect the uniqueness of our Galway Culture and richness, vitality and diversity.

I was commissioned to write a poem which the committee may look to have me read during the visit of the judges to Galway. (They didn't). The River Corrib flows through Galway and I suspect this had some tenuous connection to the overall theme of the bid which was called 'making waves', which could be represented through language, landscape or migration.

Letting the title 'Capital of Culture' and the theme 'making waves' invade my thoughts, did eventually trigger something in me – albeit perhaps not quite what the committee may have had in mind. The blank page was my biggest enemy here. The more I thought of the commission the more frustrated I became. I was never going to abandon my grain of truth, which to me is an important element in most poems. Eventually I did write the commissioned poem. I called it "Our Killer City." It ran to six pages carrying my grain of truth over the hill and under the bridge. I didn't feel compromised.

Over the top satirical poems have their own truth too; let's not be deceived by the surreal. You can hide a lot behind a word or a stanza but equally you can find a lot. A banjo of vowels and consonants can throw up a hell of a mixed grill, but go easy on the brown sauce.

I like to write by hand first. I would never show this part of the process to anyone. This is the roughest part; it allows me to get all the innards into the bowl. These are what I want the poem to express. If I had to name it I would call it the inner substance, or structure. I don't always know what I want to say, I might just have an idea that I have yet to tease out or develop. Tangents are allowed, but give them back up, don't leave them hanging there with no function like a gone off appendix.

The inner structure of a poem acts a bit like the skeleton of the poem, against which all sides of the poem have to cling. It is the heart of the poem, and if it is well built it will always hold. Poems should challenge but you should not have to do research to get the gist of a poem. People are sometimes afraid to analyse a poem in case they get it wrong. There is no wrong there is only ambiguity. When I look back at the hand written version, the first draft it is often nothing like the published version in the poetry magazine or journal.

I am convinced that all subjects are fit for poetry; everything is usable, the unsayable, the unthinkable, even the subverted cliché has standing room, everything - save the Lofty. I prefer a living language, the language of the street. Glitter is for Hollywood. Let the poems have sound and sense or sound and no sense, as is sometimes the way when you embrace tangent. Words work on their own steam; language is malleable and well able for anything that you can throw at it. Throw a chair at a word and it will still be a word. Use a trowel on a poem and you will definitely kill it. It's easy to make up words that will easily be linked to existing ones, you can own them. Readers of poetry will get it. I like to salute the spoken word poets they have their ears to the sound.

Our Killer City

Galway's bid to win Capital of Culture
is all twenty twenty give the horse plenty.
We're in with a great chance,
until they hear about
the legionnaire's disease outbreak
in the fire station,
where our lifesavers need saving.

The birds are tweeting
about the arrival of the jury this July.
The word is out they'll rule on the bid.
Best to keep them councillors out of sight,
with the malarkey they go on with, in city hall.
Govern, govern my arse.
They wouldn't govern a sly fart on a runway.
We'll end up crowned the capital of fools.
Accusations of nepotism, potassium,
a host of other isms, chisms, chasms and schisms.
I sent you that letter by mistake
said the CEO, buckling under pressure.
You are not actually co-opted
onto those committees,
FYI, you are co-workered off.

My ogyny, your ogyny, misogyny.
We laugh about it at bus stops.
We say, aren't some of our
elected representatives a laughing stock.
We'll never get Capital of Culture
if they look through that window.

Some people live their lives
so they can die on a trolley
in Galway's A&E.

Just wait and wait and wait
and you'll die waiting.
Eighteen million on a new block
and not a new bed in sight or on site.
The car park police in the hospital grounds
are a culture shock unto themselves.
Don't die on a trolley in the bidding city,
the forbidding city,
before you have paid your parking
or we will kill your next of kin
with the weight of their parking ticket.
Culture Capital or no Culture Capital.

The swans in the canals all know,
we underpay our nurses
we underpay our teachers
we overpay our consultants
and we don't know why.
This is fair-play city, or unfair-play city
if you are a woman working for years in NUIG
and hoping for a promotion.
Hashtag-go-Micheline-go.
They'll sue the blog off ya,
but won't they look silly,
don't they look silly.

This is pity city, shitty city.
Sewage in your nostrils city.
This is Galway
city of expert panels.
City of slickers and slackers
who name-call Travellers knackers.

If you want the odour of outrage
ask the students at GMIT
who have to re-sit exams.
Allegations of cheating.
Oh no not this again.
They are coming in July to rule on the bid.
We'll hide that bit of news about the GMIT
and the gender discrimination in NUIG
in the parlour that never gets used.
To that we'll throw the new block,
the bed-less block at University Hospital Galway.

This is Galway slicker and slacker.
Have your home burgled
by your favourite nephew,
while you are at his other aunt's funeral.
He didn't know it was her house
and he didn't know taking her jewellery
without her permission was stealing.

This is Galway the bidding city,
the forbidding city.
Where the woman in court apologised
to her man for putting him through this.
The judge asked her, did he apologise to you
when he was sticking that screwdriver
in your forehead?
No but he wasn't feeling himself that day
your honour.
Someone in City Hall, not a councillor this time,
is yowling about the Capital of Culture bid.
If the bid book isn't ready on time
says the yowler,
I'll send you all to the fire station
or The Picture Palace.

She is pepping and prepping and side-stepping.
Her side-kick got side kicked. No impact.
Complaining is the devil's work.
Stick in a few more theatres
that we don't have, stick in a gallery or two.
How will they know if it's true?
How will they know if it's not true?

This is Galway, city of tools.
A man brings a cleaver into hospital with him.
The judge coming down with a migraine,
reached into her bag-a-yokes.
What got into you, she said,
pleading with the plaintiff?
I heard the chops were tough your honour,
nothing more, nothing less.
But you were seen chasing the back
of a poor man's head, with a cleaver.
It wasn't me your honour, and he wasn't poor.

What about local artists?
Someone dared to ask,
not the yowler from city hall
or her side-kicked side-kick.
To hell with local artists
what do they bring the city?
Nothing but scruffy dogs
and ripped jeans,
hippies with hobbies the lot of them.
As for the buskers, wanting to fit in
with the odour of outrage.
Move them on, hide them in GMIT,
or The Picture Palace.
Don't mention local artists at all.

Let it be like they don't exist.
Raise the rents is the best way
to keep the ripped jeans gang out,
like it's always been.
Artists me arse.
This is Galway, the bidding city
the forbidding city.
City of thieves or is it scribes or is it tribes?
The jury are coming this July,
the word is out they'll rule on the bid,
for Capital of Culture
twenty twenty
give the horse plenty.
We have a great little city here,
a pity little city, a shitty little city.

The Seamstress
with the Syntax

I went to The Galway Writer's Workshop in the early eighties. My children were then aged two and four and a half years. It was there that I met Jessie Lendennie. The workshop was held in The Women's Club in the grounds of University College Galway. I loved the workshop. It was an exciting new experience as well as a social occasion.

It all started off in a kind of two-speed paddle, which suited this x-tuberculin. People strolling in around eleven am. Tea and coffee was always on the go. You were never rushed when you were reading your poems or stories.

It was very bohemian with Jessie sitting there with her needle and thread making dresses. Fred Johnston sometimes brought in his black Labrador who sat quietly under the table while we read.

Then when the constructive criticism started it all moved up a gear. It then turned into the most stimulating few hours. Nouns, verb, adverbs were pulling me into the vortex. The bohemian seamstress was on top of every poem, she knew when something didn't work and she suggested a different route to take to get a better poem.

The prose group were in the next room. Trish Fitzpatrick's Geordie accent and laughter could be heard through the thin walls. Mary Dempsey would stroll in and out of the two rooms. I thought she was in charge somehow, with her air of confidence.

I was aware that Jessie and Mike Allen had started up this workshop and Salmon Poetry. I remember Jessie's son Tim, who was twelve years old then, reading a poem called "Snow". This day Fred read a poem called "The Boar Hunt" and in a few short months his poem would be published in *The Salmon Journal*, a magazine produced by the workshop and edited by Jessie and Mike. Mary Dempsey and Mícheál Ó Riada co-edited some issues.

Mary Dempsey remained a long-time friend as did Jessie. Most of the workshop would go to Trish Fitzpatrick's house in Moycullen for barbecues during the summer and we'd go to Annaghdown to Jessie's place for laid-back social occasions.

Jessie would always say to me, yes you can say that, yes you can write that and yes it works. She was very encouraging and she always took something positive from what I wrote. I would go away and write and rewrite like a demon until the following Saturday.

In a few months I would have my very first poem published in *The Salmon Journal*, that was in June 1982. The poem was called "Dog is Dog is Dog".

Jessie wanted desperately to publish good writing and establish a publishing house in the West. Soon she would become the sole director of Salmon Publishing. That was pretty early on in Salmon's history.

Well-known local and international artists did the artwork on the covers, artists like John Behan, Brian Bourke, Padraig Reaney and Ann Costello.

My daughters remember me taking them to Jessie's house in the Claddagh. This was post-Annaghdown. Jessie and I sitting at the table that was littered with copies of poems and the room was full of books. As well as that, Eva Bourke and I used to attend a separate workshop in Jessie's house in the late eighties and we have the photos to prove it.

There was no one publishing new writing in the West

before Salmon. It was an exciting time. Eva Bourke's *Gonella* was the first book of poems published by Salmon in 1985. I followed with *Goddess on the Mervue Bus* in 1986.

Shortly after this I started to get invitations to give public readings and prison readings. I loved the idea of travelling and having your flight paid for. The idea of staying in a nice hotel was completely alien to me. Prior to me starting writing I had never been anywhere. Meeting that small group of people in the first workshop on the grounds of the college put me on a different path in life.

Looking Out from the Fog

He was an awful liar.
He said they took out his tubercular gland
and hung it on a tree to dry.
No one else said things like that,
it gave us a laugh at the wall.
We were the last of the
leaners-and-blamers-gang.

Gussie owned the tubercular gland story,
and all stinking liver, big small
and middlin' sized tape-worm
in the intestine stories.
He could weave us a lonely streak
with his war and loss stories,
that would make us nearly cry.
And we were big men.
Well some of us were big
most of us were shrinking,
from getting a taste of nothin' these days.

The amount of times he got thrown down
a well and left for dead in his stories
was not funny but we laughed
as we leaned and blamed.
Gussie was a spitter
as well as a leaner and blamer.

He used to say, cross yourself thrice
if you see a suitcase bobbing in the canal.
Like, when were we going to see a suitcase
bobbing in the canal?
He had a whole charm bracelet of weather stories.
He didn't like fog, any other weather
the body can beat he'd say.

But the fog mangles the lungs
like a net curtain jiving with wasps.
He had a thing about lungs.
Wasps he could take or leave.

With fog you don't know who your enemy is.
You don't know where he's been
before he went in.
Is he just a man of fog
or a man looking out from the fog,
or is he a spectre from the suitcase
bobbing in the canal?
With most stories we'd laugh,
with this one we didn't.

Lake Garda

We were excited, a whole week in Lake Garda, including a day trip to Venice and Verona. My daughter Jennifer and I travel well together, we have done it before. We can't do the lying on a beach for a week type holiday, so this is exactly what we wanted. A very early flight meant an overnight stay in a hotel at the airport, we secured this with car parking for eight days thrown in. Bhí muid ar muin na muice, we were on the pigs back. We started sending photographs home from the hotel in Dublin, the holiday starts here. JJ as we affectionately call her with big chicken burger, me with serious face. I was being myself, she was acting the maggot. We stayed awake too long and in the end we just waited for the 4.30 alarm call which never arrived. We made a run for that shuttle bus at 4.45 am, not laughing now, but sniping at each other. I told you to set the phones as well. Set your own phone the next time, I'm not your phone slave. The airport was thronged with August holiday makers, it was 5 am. The queues were long and one sided and seemed pointless to me, could we not run under? If you do it mam that's it, I mean it. We decided to leave the long queue and go play with the Aer Lingus ticket machine, it was easier that we thought. Boarding cards in hand we got into another long queue for security, it had the same oddness, a long walk up this way and a longer walk down that way. She snarled at me, get rid of that water, I will if I want.

We arrived at Milan Linate airport at around 10.40 local time. All safely on the bus and ready to go, or nearly ready to go. Why are we sitting here waiting? One passenger missing. After a half an hour or so we see him arriving with our guide. His bag was lost. We were all sympathetic when we heard this, before this we were all muttering, there's always one. You don't pick the group that you travel with on a package holiday neither do you the pick the hotel if you book last minute on line. Before we got to the hotel we had one ten minute stop for a coffee and a toilet break. One smoker had another and another and the guide said sharply, there are 48 people on the bus waiting for you. Her rage palpable, herself and her husband got back on.

One half of the group was dropped at what seemed like a very handsome building, it didn't look like a hotel but it had an individual sophistication. I said to JJ, I'll bet its covered in Italian marble. That was not our hotel. It was now three hours since we left the airport and so far, all we have seen is motorway. Our hotel looked like half a house that had seen better days, it had three non-descript steps that led to the foyer, a foyer that had no elegance of any type. my heart sank and I wondered about D.H. Lawrence's argument that 'instincts and intuitions are more important than reason'.

A young g woman approached us and said, your rooms aren't ready but you can leave your bags there and if you like. There was no lift so we headed up to the second floor dragging our luggage behind us. We finally got to our little cube of a room, it had two beds that resembled cots, they were as near attached as possible. You could fit a hairclip between them. Our clothes were wet with perspiration, JJ put on that air conditioner like a good daughter. I would if I could, she said but there is none. The shower worked and it didn't work depending on how you held it. The fittings had come away from the wall and the shower lead dangled there like a desperate reptile, it gurgles and spluttered then it died momentarily. The toilet was literally at the end of the bed, it had a sliding door that did not quite fit, it also had a gap underneath big enough to fit a fat child. The curtain in the bedroom had been pulled in the way that the shower curtain was pulled in the film Psycho, just that this curtain was half way down. Everything seemed to be half way here. We told the rep, she says, Oh did ye not get a fan, you can rent one at reception and you don't have to pay until you are leaving. We got a fan that did not work, we got another one that did. There was only one connection point in the room and it was over the tiny ledge over the cots. The fan was put on a chair beside the bed, the lucky one would have it blowing cool air on them all night, the unlucky one wouldn't. It kept sliding off the chair as it whirred, eventually we had to turn it off or risk electrocution. Later we tried the dinner which was included. It looked like steak and gravy but it tasted like shoe leather and gravy.

Soon enough a tour guide would be pointing out the remains of Catullus's Villa in Sirmione and the sulphur Springs for healing Catarrhal conditions. We'd hear nothing about chicken pox parties here, this was a Mediterranean chasm in a lush lemon haven.

We went on a day trip around Lake Garda. Several people from our group had gone on the cable car to Peschiera on the first day, now we could see the cable car and the slice of cliff it travelled up. No cable car for us two biddies who like the grape of an evening. Everywhere was lush, the guide pointed out the lemon and olive groves. We were entering the valley of Eden. For the next week it was wonder after wonder. Our guide was on auto pilot and there was nothing we could do but try and hold onto a fact here and there about how Caius Marius settled in the fortress in Peschiera and later how Napoleon fixed his headquarters there, or how Salo sheltered Mussolini.

In Sirmione we took a trip on a speed boat, leaving behind our regular guide for now. When the driver of the boat wanted to show us anything he left the wheel to face us and he held up a laminated photograph and pointed . He showed us a photograph of a fortress that was now the sulphur baths. When he held up a photograph of Maria Callas, he pointed to the villa where she lived between 1950 and 1959. When he wanted to race the other two boats he took off like Ariel and started to skip the top of the water, laughing as he sped. I was terrified but I never let on. The woman near me reading *Fifty Shades of Grey* never looked up.

They have bears in Arco and if you are traumatised by a bear the council pay your psychotherapy bill, according to our loquacious guide. He told us about the convent there that houses the wooden statue of the Virgin Mary that dates to the 15th century. He also told us about the 'Bee-auto-bond 'where frogs are protected, it comprises of a hedge fence that stretches for miles and some class of a crossing system that allows the frogs to cross under the road without being squelched. I wondered if this was another apocryphal tale.

Another day we had a sumptuous lunch of lasagne and wine in a refurbished farmhouse in the Alps. I wondered if the guide knew where in the Alps D.H. Lawrence had placed Gerard in that jealous and insane attack on Gudrun in the penultimate chapter of *Women In Love*. He wasn't sure about that but he was delighted to show us the sanatorium In Riva Del Garda where many famous writers came for 'the taking of the waters' including Goethe, Nietzsche, Thomas Mann, Kafka, Lawrence and others.

Just when I thought things couldn't get any better we stopped for ice-cream at Gargnano where Lawrence and his wife Frieda lived for several months in 1912 and 1913, where he finished *Sons and Lovers* and started 'Women in Love' I imagined them sitting there looking out at the stunning vista wrapped on all side by mountain peaks.

We travelled on through more picturesque villages, I couldn't take in all the intriguing facts and, drowsy from the afternoon sun, I nodded off. I woke outside the hotel, our cube room with two cots and a hairclip. My heart sank. Lawrence's lines from 'The Lemon Garden' came to mind:. 'It is better to go forward into error than to stay fixed inextricably in the past'.

The Lost Land

One of the central metaphors in Eavan Boland's work is that of a Lost Land linking Irish history with her own personal experience. She had left Ireland for the first time when she was only six years old. When she came back as a teenager Dublin was a city of smithereens, where she had to collect the fragments of her life and put them together again. The head and the heart were very much affected by the six-year-old leaving home. Memories had to be gathered and sorted and decisions made about how to cope with the child's, and later the teenager's displacement. She measures the distance between the two worlds with image, metaphor and truth.

In her elegy for "The Lost Land" the young Boland speaks of herself moving between worlds. She allows us to follow that journey. She is an exile in her own place as if she had been colonised at home. That sense of displacement is a strand that is carried into individual poems and various collections. What is intriguing about Boland's work is that she doesn't focus only on her own experiences but places them in a wider context of exile. She is definitely in it, but beyond her personal horizon there are always other people saying goodbye, picking up a suitcase and leaving and maybe never coming back. They are as much in the poems as she herself. She lays out her stall, neatly, concisely, not a word goes astray: a pristine whack of an opening for all its simplicity. You can almost hear the thump of it in the first four lines. The double-spacing makes you stop and take an extra breath.

I have two daughters.
They are all I ever wanted from the earth.
Or almost all.
I also wanted one piece of ground:

The colon after "ground" tells us she is not quite finished. She's the poet, she can say more and she must tell us how important that fourth line, the wanted line is.

I also wanted one piece of ground: Not a plateau, not a field, not a boithrín, just one piece of ground. She would have ownership of a tiny plot where she might build a house for herself and her family where she would be finally rooted. She would have a foundation. When you put down bricks and mortar you are of that place in a more real way. You are not in the shadows then. When she went back to her beloved city in her late teens, she went to boarding school in Killiney and travelled back to Dublin at weekends. So the city was still only her weekend home, her Lost Land.

So I could say mine. My own.
And mean it.

How important those few words are to her? It could be the heart of the poem but the poem has two hearts. For now we are still thinking about what she wants. She might not want much but it is still a strong yearning and not that unique when you think of it. Isn't it what we all want? A safe haven to call our own, a place to create good memories for ourselves and for those we love. The poet might have lost out on a country and spent a long time reclaiming it but it will be different for her children. She will make sure that they will not be betwixt and between, that no tempest will scatter their hold on a land, on a country. There is a piece of ground that will have a foundation. Blocks will be added and it will grow into a house with curtains and furniture and things, and most of all it will be home, Heimat, Baile. They will have emotional ease in their footfall and no exile.

The poem leaps forward and now the children have grown up, they are far away from her at this point, one still at school in Dublin. *The Lost Land* was the first book that Eavan published after moving to California to work at Stanford. The poet is looking back at the country that meant so much to her. The dislocation is almost complete when memory itself becomes an emigrant. Memory is all we have to draw the picture together in our minds, we rely on memory as our fall-back position but this is not the case here where memory is roaming around a patch of earth, an unreachable but much-loved landscape. The metaphor has nowhere to go because we are swept along with the storyline.

Then the other heart of the poem comes into play. The poet has always had a strong connection to landscape, real or imagined but mostly real, painfully real. She does not use landscape as merely a vista to be admired. It becomes more than the place we leave from, or the place to sail back to. Landscape is the canvas, sometimes empty, sometimes populated. Always there.

> Now they are grown up and far away
> and memory itself
> has become an emigrant,
> wandering in a place
> where love dissembles itself as landscape:

The straight-talking of the opening lines allows us to engage with the personal, but that is just a preamble for something much deeper. The poet goes on to weave her own life and her country's history of emigration seamlessly together. You can hear her distinctive voice when you are reading it.

At night,
on the edge of sleep,
I can see the shore of Dublin Bay,
its rocky sweep and its granite pier.

Is this, I say
how they must have seen it,
backing out on the mail-boat at twilight,

She is thinking about the people who left on the mail-boat and how they viewed that selfsame landscape that she viewed. She thinks of them and their loss, backing out, waving to loved-ones at the pier perhaps. She does not need to say too much here. She has created the scene and she lands it with a perfect pitch. I read a piece by her once* where she said: "some territory that can never be claimed, held, kept, has for me, become more enduring than any of the places I've called home." To the poet the lost land does not mean one thing, it holds a variety of meaning. A deeper meaning than a mere country, a landscape. The lost land takes in all the losses the poet has ever experienced. The losses are viewed from whatever side of the Atlantic she happens to be on. She holds a tight reign on those losses but inevitably they dissipate and all she can do now is name them. Whether she does it with elegance or grace or with a darker motif, the result is still the same.

I see myself
on the underworld side of the water,
the darkness coming in fast, saying
all the names I know for a lost land.

Ireland. Absence. Daughter.

---

* *Don't Ask Me What I Mean. Poets in Their Own Words*, edited by Clare Brown and Don Paterson. Published by Picador.

Capital of Cock-a-leekie Inferno

9 circles of 2020 Hell (with apologies to Dante)

Roll up roll up
at The Fighting Inn Café.
Get your projects in for the Bid Book.
You'll be lashed with cash
but never with Ashe.
(Buzz words: Legacy conference.)
Where we are, where we were
and where are we going,
and where can I cash that?
Barrels, trucks
and three bags full.
Life in Galway
will never again be dull
only always full, three bags full.

Incalculable groups went in –
theatre companies walked
miles in their bare feet,
Circus, Film, Music, every class of arts group.
Wearing only loin cloth and hope.
(Buzz words: money to burn)
Painters, poets, and those with
a passion for purple prose
didn't see an obvious opening.
But still they joined the ranks
of the queues that rose and rose.
They threw their pens and paint brushes
into the ring. Two by twos.
A circle was made and it was
full to the gullet with promises.
That was circle one.

Only eight more circles to go.
The Bid Book was there
with a ribbon on its cover
and big bucks tied to its bleeding spleen.
Circle seven had more ideas.
Big Car Small Shoes / Backward Motion / Ship on the Rocks
Broken Window into the West and more catchy titles.
All these ideas made the Bid Book bulge,
like a loaf caught between two slithers of ham.
(Buzz words: Project Progress how are ya?)
In circle seven the projects were oppressed and suppressed
and ready to buckle under the weight of all that creativity.
Fact: No one was driving the bus, but the bus was moving
through the streets of hell. It was not the Mervue Bus.

Circle six although now smouldering and much suffering
    had begun
and shouts of "animation and incubation"
nobody used the M word, thank God.
(Buzz words: Give good clarity, and me love you long time.)

Community engagement was on everyone's lips
but no one could speak with the flames rising up.
Then in circle five there was an announcement
through the thick walls of hell.
Fact – Creative Director Long Gone.
The experts would be called in
to fix things and tell us how to run things.
What would we know?
We're only artists after all.
(Fact or Fiction: Chaos chaos chaos.)

Some other souls not yet fully burned were shouting,
remember the famine, remember 1916
but the poor half-listeners

were blindsided by the sound of the greasy till.
The experts came from across The Wide Brexatta Sea
to design and implement our new creative strategy.
But the experts grew weary
of the cultural famine and the inn fighting
at The Fighting Inn Café,
located in circle four of 2020 inferno.

Fact: Chief Executive Gone.

In circle three they ran on the tarmac
with their pockets full, singing
Baa baa black sheep, have you any more wool?

Fact or fiction: CEO left empty-handed.

In circle two, endless gushing tributes were paid
to those who fled by those who remained.
Fact or fiction: Chair of the Board should be gone but not gone.
No leaks by the gushers about why the leavers left.
Fact: Mr X was offered the apple but the apple was
snatched from him unbitten. Job title offered, business
arrangement, directorship.
Sounds like a poem/not.

They were deserting the sinking inferno
and getting their backs slapped as they ran.
In the final circle of 2020 inferno,
the ringmasters and mistresses
using whips made from horsehair
herded all the Bid Book makers into
the hottest room in hell
and told them they had to chop
lots of percentages off their original projects.

They had experts to pay —
the ones ye were all gushing about.
They might have only stayed to hear the Angelus bell ring thrice
but they had contracts, unlike ye,
and we had money. Barrels, trucks, and warehouse loads.
Fact or Fiction: New CEO replacement is hiding in the cupboard.

Fact: Middle Island lost at sea.

Pay attention at the back and stop complaining
about your scorching eyebrows.
We are cutting everything.
Your nose hair, your toenails
but most of all your bulging budgets.
Take it and burn, or leave it and burn.

They watched the waited in the final circle
while their ankles burned.
The promised indulgences didn't work.
No one mentioned poem or painting or play
and there was no art of any kind.
No street performers. No buskers.
No songs to lighten the heart
on a dreary Galway day.
No murals to admire.
Nothing, not even a shrub
because in the ancient by-laws of 2016
shrubs were forbidden.
Any splash of colour was an affront to the senses.
Our nine circles of 2020 hell complete,
we were in the land of empty
and we were all burning like blazes.

Photograph: *Andrew Downes*

RITA ANN HIGGINS was born in 1955 in Galway, Ireland, where she still resides. Her first five poetry collections were published by Salmon: *Goddess on the Mervue Bus* (1986); *Witch in the Bushes* (1988); *Goddess and Witch* (1990); *Philomena's Revenge* (1992); and, *Higher Purchase* (1996), as well as a memoir *Hurting God* (2010). Bloodaxe Books published her next five collections: *Sunny Side Plucked* (1996); *An Awful Racket* (2001); *Throw in the Vowels: New & Selected Poems* in May 2005 to mark her 50th birthday; *Ireland is Changing Mother* (2011), and *Tongulish* (2016). Her plays include: *Face Licker Come Home* (Salmon 1991); *God of the Hatch Man* (1992), *Colie Lally Doesn't Live in a Bucket* (1993); and *Down All the Roundabouts* (1999). In 2004, she wrote a screenplay entitled *The Big Break*. In 2008 she wrote a play, *The Empty Frame*, inspired by Hanna Greally, and in 2008 a play for radio, *The Plastic Bag*. She has edited: *Out the Clara Road: The Offaly Anthology* in 1999; and *Word and Image: a collection of poems from Sunderland Women's Centre and Washington Bridge Centre* (2000). She co-edited *FIZZ: Poetry of resistance and challenge*, an anthology written by young people, in 2004. She was Galway County's Writer-in-Residence in 1987, Writer-in-Residence at the National University of Ireland, Galway, in 1994-95, and Writer-in-Residence for Offaly County Council in 1998-99. She was Green Honors Professor at Texas Christian University in October 2000. She won the Peadar O'Donnell Award in 1989 and has received several Arts Council of Ireland bursaries. Her collection *Sunny Side Plucked* was a Poetry Book Society Recommendation. She was made an honorary fellow at Hong Kong Baptist University in November 2006. She is a member of Aosdána.

www.**salmon**poetry.com

*'Like the sea-run Steelhead salmon that thrashes upstream to its spawning
ground, then instead of dying, returns to the sea – Salmon Poetry Press
brings precious cargo to both Ireland and America in the poetry it publishes,
then carries that select work to its readership against incalculable odds.'*

Tess Gallagher